Understanding the Global TV Format

By Albert Moran

with Justin Malbon

intellect
Bristol, UK
Portland, OR, USA

First Published in the UK in 2006 by
Intellect Books, PO Box 862, Bristol BS99 1DE, UK
First Published in the USA in 2006 by
Intellect Books, ISBS, 920 NE 58th Ave. Suite 300, Portland, Oregon 97213-3786, USA
Copyright ©2006 Intellect Ltd.

A catalogue record for this book is available from the British Library

Cover Design: Gabriel Solomons
Copy Editor: Julie Strudwick

ISBN 1-84150-132-8

Printed and bound in Great Britain by 4edge Ltd.

Contents

Acknowledgements

The major debt is to the Australian Research Council Discovery grant scheme for funding to support this project. When it came to the research, two people were enormously helpful in answering the many questions and helping with various elements of this book. First, Moran and Malbon recall a most pleasant conversation and lunch with John Gough in Soho on a balmy summer's afternoon. John has been extremely generous in answering various questions and helping with other matters. Second, John facilitated contact with his partner on the game show *In The Dark*, Mark Overett. Mark, too, has been very supportive in answering our numerous questions, providing further contacts, giving samples of work, speaking at workshops, and so on. It goes without saying that without the great help and kindness that John and Mark extended that this book would have been much more difficult to research and write.

In turn various others in the business have also given freely of their time in granting interviews. The following are to be thanked: David Bodycombe, Mikael Borglund (Beyond), Bob Campbell (Screentime), Julie Christie (Touchdown Productions), Bob Cousins (Fremantle), Tim Clucas (Network Ten, Australia), Jason Daniel (Fremantle), Eugene Ferguson (Granada), Christof Fey (FRAPA), David Franken (formerly Seven Network, Australia), Bill Grantham, Stephanie Hartog (Fremantle), Hugh Marks (Nine Network, Australia), Peter Meekin (Nine Network, Australia), Michel Rodrigue (Distraction), Dennis Spencer (Southern Star Endemol), Geoff Stevens (TVNZ), Lisette van Diepen (Endemol), and Joris van Manen (De Brauw, Blackstone, Westbrok).

Thanks also to Moran and Malbon's institutions – the School of Arts, Media and Culture and the School of Law at Griffith University. Grateful appreciation to various research assistants – Kate Hynes, Mark Ryan, David Adair and Tiziana Ferrero-Regis – who have helped us at various points in time.

Finally thanks also go to Manuel Alvarado and to Masoud Yazdani and May Yao at Intellect.

Glossary

Bible once this TV industry term referred to demographic, ratings and other scheduling information regarding a programme. It now refers to the total set of written information and instructions covering the adaptation of a TV format. Sometimes known as a production bible or kit.

Brand the commercial aura or buzz that surrounds a company or a product.

Broadcast rights this is the power to permit the authorized broadcast of a programme. Usually, a licensing agreement will involve two airings of the programme or episode.

Consultancy an on-the-spot mentoring and advisory service provided to a new licensed adaptation of a particular format. It generally entails a producer or another executive spending time with the production team involved in the new adaptation advising and helping to solve problems as these arise.

Copyright this provides the creator of an original work an exclusive right to print, copy, transform to another medium, translate, record or perform or otherwise use or not use the work. It also permits the creator to sell, license or distribute the work.

Creatives those individuals and groups involved in the devising and development of TV formats. In effect, their job is to think up new TV programmes.

Developer sometimes known as a 'hired gun', this is the figure or agency that expands on an initial format idea, turning it into a paper format.

Development the stage in the manufacturing of a format between devising and the broadcast of a format-based programme. Here a format idea is elaborated leading to the appearance of a paper format.

Devising the first stage of the format manufacturing activity wherein a format idea is originated and a very short draft committed to paper.

Devisor a term used as a catch-all for the writers, authors and creators that have an initial format idea. Depending on a devisor's industry experience, s/he might be able to take the idea forward into the development stage.

Distribution this is the activity of publicly circulating goods and services both to immediate users and also to potential users in other places. As the middle stage in the chain of commercial activity, this has the capacity to control both the production and consumption ends of the cycle.

Format (noun) essentially, this is the total package of information and know-how that increases the adaptability of a programme in another place and time.

Format (verb) the activity of systematically documenting and organizing together those elements that will increase the adaptability of a programme. To format is to arrange together the different parts of a format. One of the subsidiary actions involved here may include obtaining copyright clearance on particular materials to be included in the package.

Franchise a business arrangement between a licensor and a licensee whereby the former distributes a product or service in a territory using the latter as its agent. Depending on what is being distributed, the trade now distinguishes between product franchising and business-format franchising.

Intellectual property this describes a legal right to non-tangible property relating to an invention or creative endeavour. The legal rights include copyright, patents and trademarks.

Joint venture agreement a formal partnership between two organizations frequently originating in two different markets that agree to work together as equals in a third marketplace.

Moral rights additional rights attaching to the creators and authors of copyright material. These include the right of attribution or acknowledgement. These also provide for objection to any distortion, mutilation or modification of their work, or to any other derogatory action prejudicial to honour or reputation.

Paper format a written document, running six to ten pages, that outlines in detail all the key components of a programme and the manner in which these come together. Previously, this was often referred to simply as the format although, increasingly, the full term is now being used.

Passing off a legal action that can be taken against business competitors that produce a show or other product that misleads others into believing that it has been produced with your approval.

Patent a monopoly right during the patent period to prevent anyone making, using or exploiting the invention without permission.

Pilot a common term in the broadcasting industry that refers to the production of a trial or sample programme of an intended series. It serves the double function of allowing producers and broadcasters to gain a clear idea of what written material will look and sound like. Such a production also functions in term of problem spotting and solving.

Pitch (verb) to pitch a format idea to a producer or broadcaster is to set out, in broad outline only, the principal ideas for a format or a programme.

Radio format this is the creation of a deliberate form and style that enables a distinctive branding of a radio station. A particular format will operate at both the overall and the minute-to-minute organizational levels of a station or network. At the former, it identifies the broad style that the station has set such as Golden Oldie, Country Rock and so on while at the minute-to-minute level it refers to the scripting of music, talk, jingles and even commercials that maintain and extend the broad style.

Show-reel a kind of video commercial on behalf of a format prepared by the devisor and/or the developer. Its target audience is potential investors and broadcasters.

Television format although the term is understood in slightly different ways in television, we use it to mean that total body of knowledge systematically and consciously assembled to facilitate the future adaptation under license of the programme. Somewhat confusingly, the term is also being used generically to refer to some of those knowledge components such as the format bible and the paper format.

Trade association a grouping, usually voluntary, of those engaged in a particular kind of business or commercial endeavour. Membership may be individual or corporate. This coming together occurs to enable the group to better represent its collective interests to the world.

CHAPTER 1

Introduction

... television's going through a very, very difficult time, and I think we are looking at a really struggling set of programmers and programming and schedulers and executives desperately, desperately every morning waking up and thinking, 'What the hell do I do to justify my large salary?'

Paul Watson, UK TV Producer (Anon. 2002a: 44)

Formatting is the future of TV entertainment. To an extent never seen before, broadcasters around the world are sharing ratings winning concepts and ideas via the programming 'currency' of formats.

David Liddiment, Programme Director ITV (Anon. 2002c)

I love entertainment and I really believe in entertainment, which, as it happens, is having a bit of a renaissance around the world. For a long time, it was treated as the rather tacky, red nosed, endofthepier part of the business. Nowadays, with things like Millionaire *and* Pop Idol, *that's no longer true. But I think it's important to realize that this explosion hasn't changed the rules of the game. A company like Kingworld [the US game show specialist] has been churning out shows around the world such as* Jeopardy! *and* Wheel of Fortune *for 25 to 30 years. What these shows have in common is that they're multiepisodic, easily repeatable, locally replicable and made for reasonable budgets. That's what we're looking for: shows that can play in virtually any territory in Azerbaijan or Kazakhstan, where the local TV station can make them. They can qualify for quotas [in local content] in those territories where there are quotas and hook the interests of local audiences.*

Paul Jackson, Director of International Formats and Entertainment, Granada (Anon. 2002a: 44; Granada 2003)

There is no doubt that the past ten to fifteen years has seen a dramatic and significant change in television systems in very many places in the world such that the institution and its culture finds itself in a new period or era that is marked off from the past (cf. Moran 1989; Curtin 1996; Saenz 1997; Rogers, Epstein and Reeves 2002; Dill 2003). In contrast with the present moment, earlier stages of television might be usefully designated as Live Television, Filmed-series Television and 'Quality' Television. On the other hand, the characterization of the contemporary moment as that of Multi-channel or Digital Television is suggested because of a unique intersection of new technologies of transmission and reception, new forms of financing and new forms of content that have come together in recent years. What is novel and original about this kind of television is the fact that, by the 1990s, the centralized broadcasting arrangements in country after country across the world, mostly in place with minor changes since the beginning of television broadcasting in that place, have been increasingly transformed and reconstituted. The oligopolistic model is undergoing a profound transformation. Television is rapidly becoming something else characterized by new patterns, agendas and structures. Services of every kind are rapidly multiplying so that the institution is well on the way to being the tube of plenty (Griffiths 2003).

The multi-channel landscape

Beginning in the last years of the previous century and quickening since 2000, television systems in many parts of the world have been distinguished by an ongoing reconfiguration of the institutional field. Television is undergoing a sustained shift, away from an oligopolistic-based scarcity associated with broadcasting towards a more differentiated abundance or saturation associated with the proliferation of new and old television services, technologies and providers.

In the multi-channel environment of the present and the near future, television is and will be delivered by existing and new technological arrangements (McChesney 1999; Flew 2002). Meanwhile, a transforming system also comes to provide additional services to viewers, increasingly now referred to as consumers. These data services are complementary to the information and entertainment provisions of broadcasters and are increasingly more interactive than the older services.

Television may once have been defined by an oligopoly of broadcast channels, frequently as few as one or two in any centre of population. More and more, though, it seems likely to be defined by licensed or free-to-air providers together with others as the system becomes more differentiated. The new institutional players come from within and without the sector. Thus, for example, in different European markets, there has been a significant increase in the number of television broadcasting networks on the air, public service and, especially, commercial (Blumler and Nossiter 1991; Noam 1992; Wieten, Murdock and Dahlgren 2000). Meanwhile the past twenty years have also seen the onset of satellite, cable and pay TV services (Gross 1997; Paterson 1997). New players have entered the distribution arena including companies based in the telecommunications and computer sector and newspapers (Constantakis-Valdes 1997; Shrover 1997). Meanwhile, new trade agreements seem likely to encourage other groups, both local and international, to enter the television arena.

In turn, the new multi-channel environment is served and stimulated by new distribution technologies such as satellite, cable and microwave and new computer software including the Internet. Television is also characterized by a multiplying non-exclusivity of content which is now becoming available through other modes including marketing and the World Wide Web (McChesney 1999; Flew 2002; Griffiths 2003). The convergence with computers and mobile phones yields new forms of interactivity including electronic commerce, online education and teleworking. Meanwhile, digital TV, Web TV and personal video recorders (PVRS) may further strengthen a tendency towards niche and specialized programming.

At the reception end of the reconfigured system, the television set now embraces many functions including television broadcast programme reception, off-air taping and replay of videotape, engaging in computer games, playing of DVDs, surfing across channels, telecommunicating including accessing the Internet and e-mail, using dedicated information services and engaging in home shopping. In other words, 'content' has ceased to be synonymous with the television programme and programming. Instead, it has also come to include the creation of new sequences of image and sound, availing and engaging in interactive services and the accessing of dedicated data and information (Saenz 1997).

One major consequence of these changes is likely to be a falling audience for any particular television show, no matter how popular it seems to be. With so many channels and technologies of distribution and circulation, it has been increasingly impossible for any hit show, no matter how successful, to register the kinds of ratings achievable in earlier phases of television.

In turn, several responses to this situation are now evident. One of these is a stagnation, if not a drop, in the system's demand for more expensive forms of prime time programming. In the United Kingdom, for example, there has been a decline in demand for both drama and current affairs programming in prime time, a trend that has its parallels elsewhere such as Australia (Brunsdon et al. 2001; Moran forthcoming; Lawson 2002; Meade and Wilson 2001; Perkin 2001; Mappleback 1998). In other words, in characterizing the present era of New Television as one of abundance, it has to be borne in mind that this tendency only occurs with certain programming genres, indeed it occurs at the expense of other types of content.

What then is the motor or source of this differentiated abundance that is already a central feature of the new landscape? How does it register as a phenomenon and how does it come about?

Adaptation

The most significant dynamic seems to be one of adaptation, transfer and recycling of narrative and other kinds of content (Bellamy, McDonald and Walker 1990; Pearson and Urricho 1999; Thompson 1999; Brenton and Cohen 2003; Thompson 2003). Behind this proliferation of transfers, this ever-expanding recycling of content, is a set of new economic arrangements designed to secure a degree of financial and cultural insurance not easily available in the multi-channel environment of the present. Adapting already successful materials and content offers some chance of duplicating past and existing successes. Media producers, including those operating in the field of television, attempt to take out financial and cultural insurance by using material that is in some way familiar to the audience (Fiddy 1997; Moran 1998). Having invested in the brand, it makes good business sense to derive further value from it in these different ways (Todreas 1999; Bellamy and Trott 2000; Rogers, Epstein and Reeves 2002). And, of course, in turn, this tendency of recycling is further facilitated by the fact of owning the copyright on the property in the first place.

In the age of Multi-channel Television, there is a clearly identified need to derive as much financial mileage out of an ownership as possible - hence the idea of Intellectual Property. This move to safeguard and control content related ideas formalizes ownership under the protection of property laws such as those of trademark, brand name and registered design as well as those of copyright law

(Lane 1992; van Manen 1994; Moran 1998; Freeman 2002). Indeed, this era of television may come to be characterized as one of a heightened awareness and emphasis on programme rights.

The interests in rights held by television companies - both producers and broadcasters - who have joined the newly formed, Cologne-based Format Registration and Protection Association (FRAPA), discussed in more detail in Chapter 8, are not defined abstractly but change with commercial circumstances. Thus, for example, the income generated from the licensing of a TV programme into public usage has to be measured against its use as a means of promotion. As Frith has pointed out, copyright is generally used to make money rather than to control use (1987: 57-75).

Nevertheless, this emphasis on rights helps secure the general conditions for the process of selling the same content over and over again across a series of different media that has already been mentioned as a key feature of the present epoch. In the particular case of Multi-channel Television, the process of worldwide geographic dispersal and recycling of existing content goes under the specific name of TV format adaptation.

Understanding the Global TV Format serves as an introduction to the world of TV programme formats. We offer this book as a guide to the realities of this rapidly growing area of international television. This book is offered as a guide to the realities of this rapidly growing area of international television. It can be read by the general public and by the TV industry alike for insight and detail as to just how this particular kind of television works. For the trade, including those that seek to join it, it acts as a handbook, explaining in detail the elements of the business, including its legal interface, and how these function together. Meanwhile, for the general reader, and not least the keen student of what happens behind the television screen, the hope is that these pages will provide greater information, insight and understanding about this newest element of the larger international television industry and culture. For the critical reader, the book also functions to introduce inquiries and debates that Moran and others take up elsewhere. For the fact is that just out of sight so far as formats are concerned are complex questions of history, matters of aesthetic and semiotic theory, issues regarding intellectual property, changes in the institutional fields of media and business, and so on. The fact that these larger conceptual issues are not given sustained attention in these pages does not mean either that I am oblivious to these or that I do not regard them as important. However, as *Understanding the Global TV Format* is an introduction to the field, such an investigation is postponed until another occasion.

Instead, as a means of setting the scene for what follows, it is worth briefly attending to some facts and figures about the global trade in TV programme formats. Although not concerned with the fine detail of the financial ledger, which is constantly changing, rarely discloses specific details and costs and - in any case - is almost never adjusted to take account of changing currency values, audience size and so on - nevertheless, some details that help to give a broad picture of the recent explosion in the TV programme format business can be cited here.

For example, following earlier success in the United States of such UK-originated formats as *Survivor*, *Who Wants to be a Millionaire?* and *The Weakest*

Link, the American version of *Pop Idol, American Idol,* turned out to be just as popular. In late 2002, the first part of the two-part final attracted 20.4 million viewers. This made it the most watched show on News Corporation's Fox TV network that year and won its devisor, Simon Fuller, a UK pop music impresario, an invitation to the White House to meet the President. It was estimated that he would net £10m. from the US format sale and an additional £30m. from sponsorship, phone voting lines and star royalties (Australian Broadcasting Corporation 2003).

Meanwhile, from that other great European incubator of TV formats, The Netherlands, came the *IQ Test.* Devised by Amsterdam company Eyeworks, the programme first aired on Dutch television in 2001. A live, interactive programme, the format invites the nation to test its own knowledge concerning such categories as intelligence, sex, health or even humour. In Britain on the BBC the programme was branded as *Test the Nation* while on Australia's Nine Network it was known as the *National IQ Test.* Both broadcasters who carried the programme reported outstanding ratings as the studio audience and the viewing public completed detailed questionnaires that were then scored. In Britain, the format adaptation attracted more than nine million viewers while in Australia more than 3.1 million tuned in, easily the biggest single audience that year. Elsewhere in the world, the format has been remade in over eighteen other territories usually with the same remarkable success (Cozens 2003; Eyeworks 2003).

It is also worth adding here a note about Endemol, the world's largest format specialist (Anon. 1994a; Bell 1994; Briel 2001). It, too, hails from The Netherlands and was, briefly, a partner with Eyeworks. Thanks in part to the global success of its *Big Brother* format, it has become the most successful format producer and distributor in the world.

Since mid 2000, the company has been part of the Telefònica group. Telefònica S.A. is by far the largest telecommunications service provider in the Spanish and Portuguese-speaking world. In the first half of 2004, Endemol announced that it had established a Global Creative Team (GCT) to further boost its position as the world's biggest independent creator and producer of content for television and interactive platforms. The grouping brings together the company's top creative and commercial brains from across the world, and is the first stage of far-reaching new plans being introduced by Endemol's new CEO and President Joaquim Agut even as company co-founder John de Mol was stepping down. Agut commented:

> *Creativity is top priority in our company. This powerful fusion of creativity and commerce heralds a new dawn in the Group. Until now, we've never truly fused our many local creative strengths with our overall group expertise and international commercial opportunities* ('Endemol boosts creativity with Global Creative Team' http://www.endemol.com).

Conscious of the need to continue to generate new content for their broadcast and interactive systems, including the generation of new formats, the GCT will be empowered by extra funding and a state-of-the-art Intranet system called Premier 2.0 that will allow Endemol companies in 23 countries to exchange promos, pilots, format developments and treatments (Endemol 2004).

However, rather than continuing to quote facts and figures that are soon out of date, one might briefly consider another yardstick concerning the recent multiplication in the international TV programme format business. This has to do with the BBC and its decision to set up a format licensing division. Since its establishment in 1926, the British Broadcasting Corporation has found itself acting as de facto broadcasting parent to many public service radio and television organizations in different parts of the world including countries in the former British Commonwealth, Japan, Europe and even the United States. As part of this relationship, many BBC programmes have been borrowed, adapted and remade in these other territories, frequently with the British organization deriving no fees or revenues for originating the prototype or template (Jarvis 1996). Take, for example, the case of the BBC's *Tomorrow's World* and its remaking in Australia. The latter that concerned new developments in the area of science and technology had originally gone to air in the United Kingdom in 1965. In turn, without any licensing arrangement, the Australian Broadcasting Commission adapted the programme and the local version of the programme, a kind of current affairs science and technology programme, went to air in 1967 as *The Inventors* (Inglis 1982: 377-78). In 1980, the Australian public broadcaster decided to revamp this as *Towards 2000.* However, four years later, it cancelled the series for budgetary reasons whereupon several of its production team decided to go independent and to package the programme, now known as *Beyond 2000.* The programme was sold locally to the ABC and did enormously well internationally (Cunningham and Jacka 1996: 106-7). However, in all of this, the BBC derived no fees or other revenues for having originated the format in the first place. So, to help counter this kind of drain of potential revenues from adaptations, the Corporation established its own Format Licensing division inside its marketing arm, BBC WorldWide, in 1994 (Jarvis 1996; Moran 1998, BBC WorldWide 2002/3).

About this book

Given these developments in the global environment of the TV programme format trade, there is, then, no doubt about the need for a systematic overview of this relatively new face of international television. In this first English-language book devoted to the culture, business and legal dimensions of TV programme formats, I am concerned to shed greater light and understanding on the trade in all its facets and ramifications. To do this, a close liaison has been developed with different companies and individuals working in the business. Frequently, too, I have taken the word of these in terms of their understandings, rule of thumb definitions, yardsticks of judgment and so on. Such a liaison is, of course, dangerous, in terms of the self-serving and mythologizing that can occur but I believe the risk has been worth taking in order to achieve a sharper focus on what is going on.

In order to explain the subject - what constitutes a TV programme format, what does it mean and how does it work? - the pages that follow sees the book focus on three particular realms. The first of these has to do with the evolution of formats, the means and contexts in which they come about. In a classic case of mistaking the trees for the wood, recent critical research has done much to illuminate the advent of several genres of TV programme formats, most especially that of 'reality' TV, but has for the most part neglected the institutional conditions of their development and exchange (Johnson-Woods 2002; Brenton & Cohen 2003; Murray & Ouelette 2004; Mathijs & Jones 2004).

Secondly, the book is concerned to understand these mechanisms in a broader, international business context. Here, I am particularly interested in the recent and on-going transformation of television industries that is occurring across the world under the impact of TV formats. However, if these commodities have economic and cultural clout, the programmes based on their adaptation are also open to imitation and copying by anyone who watches a format adaptation on a television screen. Thus, Chapter 9 and 10 examine the different legal ways in which format holders attempt to ensure maximum financial rewards for their properties.

A glance at the contents section of the book shows that these larger subjects form the basis of several individual chapters. It is, therefore, worth setting out the sequence of these in more detail.

Chapter 2 takes up the matter of what is meant by the term 'format' as applied to TV programming. By way of spelling this out, I discuss the concept in detail, and provide a historical background before identifying the various elements that are part of a format package. Meanwhile, Chapter 3 takes up the story of where formats come from. Although format devising might be said to be an inward act of creation, nevertheless various stages and strategies for developing the bare bones of a format and then laying flesh on these can and are identified and discussed. In addition, an appendix is provided where a professional TV game show advisor sets out the concrete steps whereby a format for a television quiz show is brought into existence. Several formats in both their short, outline form and in longer, fuller, more detailed style are discussed at some length in this chapter (as well as in Chapters 4 and 5) so that although this is not a 'how to' book, nevertheless the reader gains a much clearer understanding about how formats are composed and produced. In short, taken together, these will help the reader get a better grasp on this part of the process.

Moving towards an engagement with the broader dimensions of the business, Chapter 4 addresses the subject of format development, the act of turning what is still mostly a private idea or set of ideas, perhaps in the mind of one or two people, into something that is more developed, more substantial and more open. In fact, this movement is part of the act of going public so that this story leads into the next chapter that is concerned with programme format distribution. Here, I seek to emphasize the singular fact that the programme format business is only incidentally to do with television. Instead, the circulation of TV programme formats is a franchising operation where what is licensed between parties is a set of services rather than a material or tangible product.

The larger, international business environment of formats becomes the basis for the next three chapters. Chapter 6 looks in more detail at the markets and other mechanisms that facilitate the international distribution of formats. Like TV programme formats themselves, the markets are a very important means whereby television companies in different parts of the world are brought together and maintained as an international network. Of course, the distribution instrument that is the market has also been important in terms of helping to organize finance, production and the distribution of completed films and TV programmes over almost a half century. Nevertheless, in recent years, the fairs and festivals have also been centrally significant in the consolidation of the international trade in TV programme formats.

In turn, I survey what can be called the TV format companies, both small and large. Protecting a format against imitation and rip-off will be an ever present consideration for a devisor and developing an on-going relationship with a production company may therefore serve the double purpose of helping to bring a format to fruition on screen and also safeguarding the property itself. Chapters 6 and 7 take this matter of going public onto an even wider stage, that of the world. More specifically, the first of these has to do with the international rounds of markets, the fairs or sales conventions that bring together those with television wares, including formats to license, and those who would deal with them, in this case potential licensees. The formatted TV programme is a global commodity and these conventions and markets are crucial mechanisms in these processes of exchange.

However, although the industry acts both in concert and also with varying degrees of friction, nevertheless it does subscribe to a belief that the format trade is a rational one and that traders mostly behave as though there is some semblance of rules and order. Chapter 8 looks at the recent emergence of a trade association that also attempts to regulate the industry that it represents. In fact, the move in 2000 to set up an industry association might also be seen as part of a larger rationalization and formalization of what had previously operated in a more ad hoc and informal manner. Hence, as a step towards broader understanding of the business, the second part of the same chapter situates the TV programme format trade alongside the business-format franchising industry. I suggest that the larger, older business has useful things to teach to the TV newcomer.

As well as relying on a battery of industry practices and a trade association as a means of guarding from unauthorized copying of format ideas, groups operating in this area also have recourse to various legal mechanisms to safeguard and protect their ideas. The next two chapters look in more detail at some of the legal mechanisms that have been, or might be, used to achieve this.

In Chapter 9, the book analyses the law regarding TV formats. To do this, I follow the course of a devisor/producer who we call Frieda who has devised a format and now seeks to both develop this with the assistance of others in the television business and, at the same time, protect the property that she has created. The chapter therefore reiterates elements already touched upon in previous chapters but this time looking at what kinds of protection the law extends to a creator in this situation. In particular, Malbon considers the specific protections that might be accorded under laws relating to copyright, contract and business reputation. Copyright is an especially important matter so that this becomes the basis for a more detailed examination that occurs in Chapter 10. Here, he is especially concerned to distinguish between whether or not a format owner has a copyright in the work and also whether the advent of a similar programme to the one based on the format constitutes a copyright infringement. These are separate matters although they are frequently confused and bundled together. Finally, a concluding chapter summarizes the main findings and claims of the book.

Four appendices follow. The first lists additional sources of information and guidance concerning the area of TV programme formats. New websites, courses and workshops and other initiatives are constantly appearing so that it is worth knowing where to turn to remain up-to-date. Appendix ii is a primer on the devising and development of new game shows written by British game show specialist David Bodycombe. It is included both because the book has touched upon some of his ideas and also because it helps to amplify my own remarks about the process of devising. An Endemol Interactive Proposal Form is reproduced as an example of a tool of the trade. It also indicates the kinds of thing that a devisor/developer needs to think about in pitching a format concept or paper format to a production company. Last of all is a breakdown of the self-identified format companies operating according to country and region that are briefly mentioned in Chapter 6. Taken together, these offer up-to-date information on local companies in particular territories and also suggest the pattern and structure of the international industry.

CHAPTER 2

Understanding the TV programme format

It is time to redefine the meaning of the word 'format', to avoid Jerry Springer claiming the format 'wild talk show'... worldwide a talk show that has four breaks in it in which the guest is confronted with dilemmas becomes a format because of the four gamebreaks, however a talk show about sex is not a format: although people think sex is a format.

Harry de Winter, IDtv executive producer (Buneau 2000: 46)

A format sale is a product sale. The product...is a recipe for re-producing a successful television programme, in another territory, as a local programme. The recipe comes with all the necessary ingredients and is offered as a product along with a consultant who can be thought of as an expert chef.

David Bodycombe, game show devisor and consultant (2002)

More and more broadcasters are required to make locally produced programming. If they don't have a lot of money to produce a lot of local fiction and drama then what do they do? They pick up a format. It's the ideal combination, you get to use creative talent and ideas from around the world and yet you still cover your need for locally produced shows.

Hayley MossBabcock, Fox World (Daswani 2002)

In the face of an increasing tendency to use the term format to refer to a form, a formula, a style, a template in a series of different fields, this chapter seeks to restrict its usage in relation to the area of TV programmes. In particular, it is the case that the term has acquired a specific meaning within the domain of international TV programme trade and this is the concern of this book. Hence, we begin our analysis by looking to define the term.

The word format has its origins in a Latin phrase (*Liber*) *formatus*, meaning a book formed in such and such a way. The first usage of the word occurs in relation to the printing industry and the book trade and concerns the shape and size of a book (*The Oxford English Dictionary* 1989: 85). Hence, a format is an alternative book size to others such as octavo and quarto. However, closer to its present usage in television industries is a more recent idea of a format being a style or manner of arrangement or presentation, a mode of procedure. Thus, the *Oxford English Dictionary* quotes the English newspaper *The Spectator* in 1958: 'The principal performer ... had to write the scripts herself and when ... she attempted to heed criticism and alter the format, she was told that the show, however bad, must go on'

(1989: 85). About the same time, the term also began to be used in connection with the newly-emergent field of information processing. Here it was applied to designate a particular arrangement of data or characters in a record, instruction, word and so on in a form that could be processed or stored by a computer (1989: 85).

Additionally, my word processor's thesaurus lists thirteen different synonyms for the term format, ranging from blueprint, through pattern and design, to model and shape. But where these terms imply a cultural meaning in designating an object that can be copied, the word format in the phrase - television format - carries a specific industrial meaning. In broadcasting first and then in television, the term has been closely linked to the principle of serial programme production. A format can be used as the basis of a new programme, the programme showing itself as a series of episodes, the episodes being sufficiently similar to seem like instalments of the same programme and sufficiently distinct to appear like different episodes. Similarly, behind industrial/legal moves to attempt to protect formats from unauthorized adaptation, lies a related notion that formats are generative or organizational (van Manen 1994: 22-7).

To put this another way, existing TV programme formats are capable of producing new elements that expand the range of possible applications or adaptations. The spin-off programme is both new and original but its seeds and potential is seen to lie in the pre-existing programme format (Gitlin 1985: 63-85; Thompson 2003: 74-105). Hence, from one point of view, the emphasis falls on the idea of a core or a structuring centre. This view is at work in accounts that sees a TV format as equivalent to a cooking recipe. Accordingly, a television format is understood as that set of invariable elements in a programme out of which the variable elements of an individual episode are produced. Equally, though, the stress may fall on the idea of the format providing an outer shell or organizing framework that permits and facilitates the making of a programme. According to this second view, a format can be understood as a means of ordering individual episodes of a programme. As a television producer once put it: 'The "crust" [of the pie] is the same from week to week but the filling changes' (Moran 1998: 13).

Other kinds of formats

As this book has already hinted, a further source of confusion to the matter of just what we mean by the term, is the fact that the name format is by no means unique to television production industries. Rather, it is to be found employed in various other sectors of communications and business. Three different instances of these usages are worth mentioning here.

First, in commercial radio programming or scheduling practices beginning in the United States in the 1950s, the term has two related and quite specific meanings. At the broad level, as a means of station branding - clearly marking one radio station out from another - the term is used to characterize the kind of programming that is being undertaken, such as Top-40, Easy Listening or All-News. Secondly, at the more local, minute-by-minute level, as a means of further consolidating this identity or station branding, the term refers to the routine, or the list of distinct ingredients, found in a programme hour. This will include specific phrases to be spoken, jingles, programme content, and the order and manner of placement (Berland 2003; Lee 2004).

Similarly, the word format is also used by writers and directors in connection with scriptwriting for film and television production. For instance, a recent book on how to write a fiction script for the big or small screen suggests that a screenplay may appear in several different formats (Armer 1998). Here, the format of a script refers to the level of detail or otherwise that appears in the finished version of the screenplay. Over and above the basic particularities concerning narrative elements and character dialogue, the format of a specific script may also include suggestions about camera angles, special effects, musical score, costume and so on. Put another way, two versions of a film script may be the same so far as narrative and dialogue are concerned although their formats may be quite different.

Finally, much more relevant to the case of TV programme formats, one can also notice the use of the term in relation to the business of franchising. Franchising is a commercial operation that orchestrates the distribution of goods and services between large-scale producers and smaller distribution agents. Where the commodity being circulated under this kind of arrangement is a non-tangible good, a kind of package of assistance in a particular area of commerce, then the trade refers to this as 'business-format' franchising (Vaughan 1979; Coltman 1988). This coincidence of meaning and application is particularly interesting and suggests that the arena of franchising is an important one in which to situate the subject of this book. I will return to a possible affinity and connection between franchising and TV programme format distribution in Chapter 8.

Collectively, these different examples of the use of the term format in areas adjacent to the present one underlines the need to be very clear about what one does mean by the label. Hence, by way of further explaining this notion, it is worth briefly looking to the past and, in particular, the evolution of the sense of the TV programme format.

Some history

Certainly there are many precedents for the practice of television programme format adaptation to be found in the development of the media. Among historical phenomena that come to mind are the redeployment of successful book, newspaper and magazine formulas in different parts of the world and the long running practice of cover versions of recordings in the music industry. Indeed, the general roots of this kind of copying or imitation - including that of TV programme format adaptation - are probably inextricably linked with the emergence of culture industries themselves after the development of the first systems of mechanical reproduction in the book trade. For example, following the birth of printing in Europe in the fifteenth century, the first printed book to appear was the Latin Bible. Nonetheless, Latin was only understood and read by a small part of the population. Therefore, to increase sales publishers had the Bible translated into several vernacular languages associated with particular regions of Western Europe. These they printed and sold. This early example of format adaptation immediately had its anticipated effect of increasing sales of the Bible among native speakers in several different parts of the region (Moran 1998).

Closer to the present, the history of, first, radio broadcasting and then early television is also littered with many examples of programme (format) adaptation. Hence, for instance, from the late 1930s onwards, Australian commercial radio had its own versions of several popular US radio network series including *Lux Radio Theatre* and *Big Sister* (Moran forthcoming). Even the BBC in 1951, paid a fee to Mark Goodson and Bill Todman, the devisors and owners of the US radio panel show *What's My Line?*, to facilitate its adaptation for, first, BBC Radio, then BBC Television (Brunt 1985). Similarly, the period of transition from radio to television that is associated with the 1950s in western countries also saw the wholesale recycling of radio programmes as the basis for new television shows.

In among these changes, some programme owners and producers were more clear-headed about the potential business principles involved. After all, incidental copying or imitation is one thing. Any programme (like any cultural artefact in general) is capable of being imitated, copied, parodied, caricatured and so on. Of course, this is not to say that such adaptation will succeed in rendering a close likeness to its original. However, systematically facilitating that adaptation is something else, a new business departure. Take the example of the children's television programme, *Romper Room* (Hyatt 1987: 364). This first appeared on a local US television station in Baltimore in 1953. The year was an auspicious one as US small business organization was beginning to undergo a transformation with the emergence of a new kind of franchising operation (Dicke 1982: 218-44). Hitherto, franchising had been organized around the distribution of material goods or products. However, in the 1950s, a new kind of franchising emerged. One of the most spectacular examples of this kind of distribution arrangement had to do with new fast food restaurant franchising including those associated with Burger King, Kentucky Fried Chicken and McDonald's (Dicke 1982).

Although the Baltimore version of the *Romper Room* programme was reasonably successful, its creators - husband and wife team, Bert and Nancy Claster - turned down CBS Network's offer to buy the programme. Instead, the Clasters licensed out or franchised the format to a string of local television stations across the country. Those that signed up to use the formula to make their own version of the programme received the rights to select and employ their own hostess and to obtain merchandise and materials representing the programme including a grinning jack-in-the-box holding a stake with the series title and Mr. Do Be, a smiling yellow jacket. Episodes were loosely structured to consist of games, book readings and other activities using a range of *Romper Room* products. As part of the franchising arrangement, Nancy Claster, who had been the original on-air hostess in Baltimore, ran weeklong courses for college-graduate hostesses who would front the programme. By 1957, 22 stations were taking the format. Six years later, 119 US stations had their own *Romper Room*, each led by a college graduate hostess. By then, too, the format was being distributed internationally and included several versions being made in Australia and Japan.

The copying of TV programmes - both authorized and unauthorized - has continued down to the present. However, for the most part, the different knowledges accumulated by the original producers remained scattered and undocumented. Instead, format knowledges had to be inferred from the residual traces available in broadcast episodes of the programme and, with fiction, from scripts. By contrast, it has only been in the recent present (some date the change to around 1990) that producers have begun to systematize and document various production knowledges that come together under the name of the programme format. Clearly, though, the seeds of this development lie back in the 1950s and 1960s with programmes such as *Romper Room*.

A multiple entity

The underlying point running through previous sections of this chapter is that a TV programme format is not a simple or even a single entity (Dawley 1994). Although the international television industry talks confidently of the format as a stand alone, unitary object, it is in fact a complex abstract and multiple entity. To underline this point, Moran has suggested that it is beside the point to look for some kind of core or essence with a format. The key question to ask is not 'what is a format?' but rather 'what does a format permit or facilitate?' (1998: 17-18). Not surprisingly, a format is, typically, seen to be manifest in a series of overlapping but separate forms. At the point of programming and distribution, it takes the cultural form of different episodes of the same programme. Meanwhile, as we shall see in the next two chapters, at the production end, it appears as a series of different but overlapping industrial entities. Somewhat confusingly, the overarching, even generic name of this package is that of the TV programme format. In fact, to take this matter a little further, one might claim that a format is a kind of abstraction known only through the various shadows that it throws although these are collectively deemed sufficient to persuade many of its actual existence. In addition, the general name of format is also attached to some of its constituents as, in part, a means of indicating that these belong to the larger package.

What then are the knowledge components of a format? Briefly, in no significant order, they can include the following elements:

1. The paper format. This has been summarized as the detailed written document that presents the initial concept for a television programme format. John Gough of Distraction Formats has usefully expanded on this: '[They] are the documents that bring content to concept. They are written as the first step in the production process for programmes of most television genres. They are written as a description of a programme's basic idea, its content, its layout and its style' (Bodycombe 2002).

2. The programme/format Bible. Although the term 'Bible' was once used to refer to ratings and demographics information, nowadays this usage has disappeared. Instead, the term refers to the total dossier of materials associated with a format. Frequently running to several hundred pages and containing some of the materials listed here, the programme or format Bible is - in effect - the total manual and reference guide to every aspect of the programme and helps answer any query regarding production, marketing, promotion, and distribution.

3. Production consultancy services. This is the provision of systematic advice and

help provided by the format licensor to the licensee. Frequently, it will involve on-the-spot guidance for a specific period, usually a week or fortnight, while the initial production of the adaptation is in progress. The consultancy will generally take the form of a senior producer from the original production overseeing and advising the early making of the adaptation. Hence, for example, King World has an executive producer associated with the game show *Wheel of Fortune*. It is her/his job to travel the world advising and helping start-ups of new adaptations of that format.

4. Blueprint and set specifications. Having these details saves on cost, enhances the format brand and helps provide part of the framework in which certain of the other elements designated here come into play. Physically, this design helps anchor the production of the format adaptation.

5. Computer software and graphics. These programmes will facilitate the efficient production of graphics, programme titles and special effects. The fact that they already exist as a template also helps in containing costs associated with this part of the production.

6. Titles. Obviously, this is one aspect of the software and graphics provided by the format licensing company. However, it is mentioned separately not least because it can form part of a branding process associated with the format and, perhaps, the company. So, the category of titles can involve trademarks, logos and written text and labels.

7. Sound. Again, there are economies involved in having selections in sound and music already in place thanks to the presence of a format. Sound may be incidental and minimal although as recent formats such as *Who Wants to be a Millionaire?* demonstrate, it may also have a more active and dynamic presence. Music can be integral and certainly theme songs and jingles are important in the format identification.

8. Scripts. These only exist in the case of formats involving 'filmed' rather than 'live' programmes. Nevertheless, in the case of formats for situation comedies and drama series, scripts of individual episodes are bearers of further production information and know-how. Typically, they help fill out the narrative situation of a series, perhaps with projected storylines, together with detailed outlines of the characters. Scripts can be used directly in a new version of a programme, can be modified or adapted to a new setting, performers or production circumstances, or may simply be available as background material. And, over and above, this kind of script, there may also be available post-production scripts that record in written form some of the sequence and detail of what has been captured on screen.

9. Dossier of demographic and ratings data. Needless to say, it is only programmes that have been successful in gathering large audiences that will be attractive for format licensing purposes. That said, the compilation of information about the scheduling, target audience, ratings and audience demographics for the formats previous broadcasts serves two functions. First, it tells the adapter more about the format, most especially about its track record and, therefore, its potential audiences. Equally importantly, the information also offers a licensee insurance of sorts for further ratings success.

10. Scheduling slots and related information. Closely allied with the previous service, this knowledge is important in further alerting the licensed adapter to various different programming possibilities. The programming history of a format in various territories constitutes an invaluable record of trialling and testing before different audiences. It is of obvious benefit for a programmer about to schedule a new version of the format.

11. Off-air videotapes of programmes. These represent full on-screen realizations of the various knowledges contained in such elements as the Paper Format, the Bible and the consultancy service. Highlighting what has been done in other territories, these recordings function much like programme pilots. In other words, they simultaneously show what the format once adapted will look and sound like and also help set a standard to be repeated and/or varied. A collection of such off-air recordings is sometimes referred to as the video Bible.

12. Insertable footage. A format may allow for or even call for filmed or videotaped segments to be integrated with new material. Hence, the same footage can turn up in both the original and in an adaptation of that format. Clearly, this can happen in several different types of formats including a game show and an anthology-type programme such as *Funniest Home Videos*.

Paper formats and programme formats

Spelling out these elements in detail as has been done here helps make the point that the term format is a complicated one and can be understood as referring to a complex, multiple entity as represented in Figure 2.1. Therefore, it is worth ending this chapter by again emphasizing the fact that a TV programme format is an interconnected parcel of particular knowledges that will be galvanised in the production, financing, marketing and broadcasting of a TV programme. Putting together a TV programme format involves a process of aggregation and accumulation that begins with a simple programme idea and ends with a full programme format. Understood in this way, there are three main stages in this cycle. The starting point is the opening idea, which is articulated as the initial paper draft. The first stage in its elaboration and organization is called devising and its end result is seen to be the production of a paper format. In turn, under the name of format development, a second cycle sees this become a broadcast programme. Finally, the last stage of making goes under the name of distribution. This

Figure 2.1 – The Format

witnesses the circulation of various accumulated knowledges under the name of the programme format.

Three written documents, the initial paper draft, the paper format and the programme format, form important reference points in this cycle. As the first of these labels imply, the paper draft is simply the committing to paper of the skeleton or barebones of a programme format notion or knowledge. We have already outlined what is meant by the second. Briefly, it is the detailed written document that fills out the initial concept for a TV programme format. To quote Gough again:

> *It is the catalyst around which all the resources that go into producing a television programme first start to gather. They develop as the production process moves forward taking into account the influences of the various production requirements such as casting, set, budget etc. evolving into the format bible and pilot programme. If the paper format is sound, the television production will be sound.* (Bodycombe 2002)

Meanwhile, at the very end of this chain of activities, the TV programme format is the accumulated store of specific information and know-how, represented in Figure 2.1, that provides the intelligence to reproduce an existing TV programme in another territory. Put another way, it is the entire body of knowledge that has been gathered through the process of putting it all together, which allows another television company in a particular territory to bypass development mistakes and pitfalls and reproduce the success of a programme that was originally made elsewhere. Michel Rodrigue, CEO of Distraction Formats explains this further:

> *[It] is a recipe which allows television concepts and ideas to travel without being stopped by either geographical or linguistic boundaries. To achieve this, the recipe comes with a whole range of ingredients making it possible for producers throughout the world to locally produce a television programme based on a foreign format, and to present it as a local television show perfectly adapted to their respective countries and cultures.* (Buneau 2001)

Holding this outcome or end result in mind, we must start our investigation of format evolution with the beginnings of the process, with the prototype, whether thought of as recipe or piecrust. It is, after all, the point from which everything else starts. Accordingly, our next three chapters take up this sequence or trail. We trace the steps whereby the move is made from initial programme idea to paper format and from there to TV programme format. The key operations that reconfigure this space are known under the specific industry names of devising, development and distribution.

CHAPTER 3

Devising a format

A format is all about the rules you put on an idea.

Julie Christie, CEO Touchdown Productions (Interview Moran 2003)

You need to be watching everything and, yes, I watch everything.

Mark Overett, Format Devisor and Executive Producer (Interview Moran 2002)

This is the first of three chapters that follow the process whereby an initial format idea is progressively matured into, a TV programme format. Elsewhere, in other accounts of how television programmes are put together, the stages of making might be identified as pre-production, production, post production and broadcast. Nevertheless, that kind of model only holds good for the making of a completed TV programme which, if given international distribution at all, will be licensed for re-broadcast in other territories. Since the mid 1970s, several media researchers have followed the making of different television programmes and Figure 3.1 offers a breakdown of the more usual stages in this kind of production and broadcast sequence (cf. Elliott 1972; Alvarado & Buscombe 1978; Hobson 1982; Tulloch & Moran 1986).

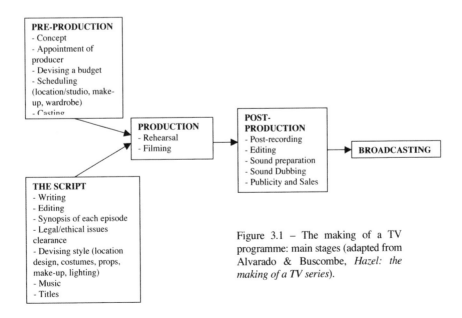

Figure 3.1 – The making of a TV programme: main stages (adapted from Alvarado & Buscombe, *Hazel: the making of a TV series*).

On the other hand, with the making of a TV programme format, the entity that comes together is both more than and different to a TV programme. Put another way, a separate object is taking shape such that the familiar phases involved in making a new programme from scratch are interrupted by a different cycle. Under this latter regime, the first broadcast of a (completed) programme based on a format is simply a stage in its elaboration and evolution. The process of concretization and refinement is, potentially at least, fairly open ended. No doubt, the format for Endemol's *Big Brother* is now many times larger and more elaborate than when in 1998 the programme first went to air in The Netherlands. And certainly, too, with its continued success in very many parts of the world, the format seems likely to continue to grow in the foreseeable future (cf. Mathijs & Jones 2004).

In other words, with a programme that proves to be at least reasonably popular in its initial broadcast, the process of documentation and format assemblage is likely to continue for some time, even while the distribution of the format is taking place in different territories. Subsequent adaptations of a format-based programme can add, cumulatively, to its system of knowledge. In short, a later version of a programme based on a format may differ from and contain more detail and know-how than an earlier incarnation.

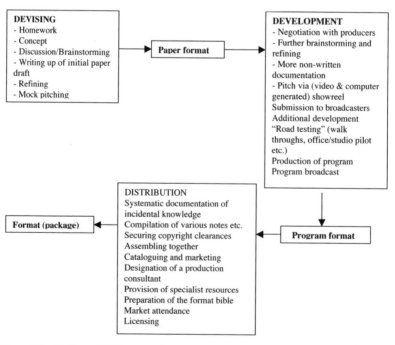

Figure 3.2 – Making a TV format: main stages

Hence, instead of the more familiar intervals and stages associated with the making of a TV programme, we here concentrate on three phases to do with devising, development and distribution (see Figure 3.2). In practice, the major stages are not neatly separated but rather tend to overlap. Moreover, the individual processes identified are very frequently repeated several times. Whether we hold to the model of the format as a cooked dish or a piecrust, it is not the case that the genesis of the dish or pie is one thing and the preparation, presentation, serving, staging and so on are another. So with formats! Execution and trialling feed back into the fuller spelling out of the format knowledges just as the latter guides and directs the TV programme's development.

Nonetheless, formats do have a beginning. Therefore, we start here with the initial idea, the basic concept, the catalyst for the programme format. Under the general name of devising, we are especially concerned with this early part of the process leading up to the writing of the paper format. And while all that happens in the making of a TV programme format (or, for that matter, a TV series) might be described as imaginative or aesthetic labour, nevertheless, the notion of creation is particularly seen as applicable to the first step in this process. In turn, the television industry gives those involved in this initial endeavour their own designation or name.

The creatives

Where, then, do format notions or concepts come from? How do they begin? The brief answer is most likely to be television itself. A fuller answer might be that these kinds of ideas seem to be 'in the air'. In particular, the thoughts, brainwaves, flashes, hunches, inspirations, mental electricity intuitions and so on that eventually trigger formats appear to come from three different social sources. These are the TV viewing public, employees within larger media organizations, and specialist 'think-tanks' set up for this purpose. Let us look at these three in more detail.

1. The audience

Fans are sometimes seen as potential creators of popular entertainment. This is well illustrated with Harlequin popular romances (previously Mills and Boon). Here, a sizeable number of fan readers have themselves become writers of romance novels. So, too, there have been moments when members of the TV viewing public have managed to cross the line, becoming generators of programme ideas rather than just consumers or passive viewers. Within the international TV format industry, there are a handful of apocryphal stories concerning a member of the public, a part of the television audience, who has had a good programme idea and has ended up devising or helping to devise a successful TV format.

Take the example of John M. Lewis (1998). Then a salesman with British Telecom, he was just one of very many who in January 1985 tuned into the BBC to watch the documentary, *Come On Down*, the programme featured Barry Norman as programme host who travels to the United States to investigate the origins of the TV game show. Here, as a kind of riposte to the BBC's commercial rivals, he discovers that most of the quiz shows still being formatted for adaptation and broadcast on British screens in the 1980s were in fact based on US originals that had first appeared in the 1950s. Watching the programme, Lewis could not believe what passed for entertainment. Britain must, he thought, be able to invent its own, infinitely better shows. In a classic instance of 'I can do better than that', Lewis set about proving that he was right.

Shortly, Lewis had come up with the idea of *Fifteen to One* (originally *Twenty to One*). An easily understood quiz or game show format had come together under his pen. In turn, using his experience as a salesman, he presented his short outline as a selling document. Finding the names of several quiz show producers from the *Radio and TV Times*, he sent off his proposal to a handful of these and waited. Four rejection letters soon came back. Two of the producers did not bother to reply. But fortunately, one producer, William G. Stewart, did. Recognizing promise in the idea, he bought a two-year option to develop the show.

Originally, the former salesman had imagined prizes, as was in vogue at the time. However, in the development process, this system was replaced by one wherein points were allocated to contestants. Otherwise, Regent Productions, who developed the format, changed very little from Lewis' original concept. The only other major change was the number of contestants used. Initially the show employed more but the group was cut to fifteen in order to help fit a half-hour timeslot. A pilot show was made and shown to Shamus Cassidy, a commissioning editor at Channel 4. He liked what he saw and the programme went into production.

All in all, to bring *Fifteen to One* from conception to its initial broadcast in the United Kingdom had taken four years. The programme first went to air in 1988 and continues down to the present. Needless to say, it has been an outstanding success with the format being adapted for other platforms including radio and in-flight entertainment. Action Time has distributed the property in other markets so that, for instance, Poland has *Ten to One*, and in Germany the adaptation was known as *Jeden Gegen Jeden* (All Against All). In turn, the format helped make Lewis a wealthy man. However, lacking any production background in television himself, his subsequent involvement with the format has been minimal.

Altogether this story is most instructive. The devisor/producer who told it to us remarked that most companies today will not respond to or even read any unsolicited format ideas. In any case, Lewis' concept probably furnished only the bare bones for a format. Channel 4 needed to put him into partnership with an experienced TV producer in order to facilitate the elaboration of the format concept. Lacking any background in television production, Lewis' involvement with *Fifteen to One* was soon at an end. He does, however, continue to receive a production credit on each episode. Significantly, though, his title there is that of Creator rather than Devisor highlighting the fact that he furnished the initial idea but played only a small part in the ensuing task of turning the idea into a TV programme format.

While there are a handful of other outsiders who have also created successful formats - notably Dr Fintan Coyle, a general practitioner again from the UK, who in association with the BBC created the game show, *The Weakest Link* - the fact is that unsolicited ideas hardly ever get past first base. The larger companies, including the broadcasters, tend towards the public proclamation that genuinely original ideas are rare and are more likely to come from inside the industry rather than from outside.

So where then does this line between outside and inside the industry run? The door is not always shut tight. Although some companies will not accept or read unsolicited format ideas or concepts others, especially small or new production companies will. One such group maintaining an open door policy is the Dublin-based Midas (Malbon 2004), while another is London-based Playbox Partnership (Goodwin 2001; Kingsley 2003). Equally, even a giant such as Endemol has in the recent past invited proposals from the public at large through an Endemol Interactive Proposal Form available on its website (see Appendix iii). In other words, although the policies of particular companies will change over time and there is a tendency not to talk with newcomers, nevertheless, there are recurring opportunities for outside ideas to find their way into larger organizations. Once inside, they may connect with experienced industry groups that will help turn them into paper formats.

2. Media personnel

Sometimes, a format may originate not among separate members of the public at large but rather on the part of an individual within a large media organization. Inside the media but outside a format company, as it were. Or even inside a format company but outside the actual job of devising and developing. Again, this is not surprising. For although such an individual may not be directly involved with creating formats, nonetheless, being located within a media organization on a day-to-day basis allows such a person to get a sense of what is topical and current. In particular, being at the format-devising coalface offers a better opportunity to spot or dream up new programme format possibilities than might be the case otherwise. To that end, media companies frequently encourage their general staff to come forward with format ideas, knowing that there are recognized procedures in place to receive and, if warranted, develop these. Hence, at Granada Television, if a format idea comes to the surface in this way, then the company will formally register the ownership of the idea. It then applies whatever development process is necessary at its own expense including brainstorming, think-tanking, piloting it, broadcasting, distributing and so on (Granada 2003).

By way of example of this kind of initiative behind closed doors, we can cite a 2002 case at Granada reported by the *Financial Times*. In that year, as part of its 'Prime Mover' initiative designed to generate new successful formats from inside the company, Granada announced the marketing of a new game show programme entitled *Win the Break*. Devised by an unidentified 'middle-ranking associate producer' within the company, the programme involved studio contestants and viewers answering questions about the programme's commercial breaks. Under a profit sharing arrangement, the devisor was due to earn 10 per cent of net profits from international sales which would fall to 5 per cent if the format earned more than £5m (Deans 2002).

Advancing still further into the media industries, we find that the likelihood of new formats being generated increases considerably. Take the case of the genesis of *Who Wants to be a Millionaire?* as outlined on the programme's website (2004).

While not directly in the business of television production, UK radio talk-back host Mike Briggs had a 'vague idea' for a new television game show which he scribbled down on a scrap of paper. As the programme's website tells it, the programme concept was developed over several lunches with writers, Steve Knight and Mike Whitehill. As it turned out, the three colleagues hammered away at the idea for three years, extending and refining, problem spotting, testing and re-testing.

As the idea progressed it became clear that the trio, by now forming the company, Celador, were on to something big. But they were still a long way from getting the programme to air. Discussions with ITV had already started. A change of ITV Programme Director and a radical overhaul of the format after a first pilot saw further revisions to the evolving format. The latter included changing the lighting, the set and the music just a matter of days before *Who Wants to be a Millionaire?* finally made its debut on ITV in 1998. (We return to this story in more detail towards the end of the next chapter.)

Similarly, Charlie Parsons had trained as a researcher with London Weekend Television before becoming a journalist with the Channel 4 current affairs program, *Network 7*. Here, in 1987, he was particularly intrigued by an item on the latter concerning a group of five people transported to a deserted island who had to cope without any of the trappings of civilization. Parsons joined 24 Hour Productions (later Planet 21) as a partner with Bob Geldorf and Waheed Ali. Thanks to the success of their *Big Breakfast*, he was in position to develop to broadcasters other programme ideas including the desert island concept. However, discussions with broadcasters about licensing the format got nowhere because the situation lacked any kind of resolution or end point. The breakthrough with the latter came once Parsons realized that having the castaways vote each other off introduced a vital story element into a format that became *Survivor*. But the UK and US broadcasters were still unconvinced. Instead, in 1997, it was Sweden that first licensed the format, making the first adaptation of *Survivor* as *Expedition Robinson* (Hazelton 2000; Brenton & Cohen 2003: 44-80).

These examples highlight two important points that are worth bearing in mind. First, following on from what we have already suggested, the fact is that format ideas are quite likely to come from inside the media industries. Secondly, on a more cautionary note, it may take a good deal of time to bring these to fruition in the shape of both a TV programme and a TV programme format.

3. Think-tanks
Clearly, new format ideas are the lifeblood of any company that works in this area. If the tendency is to shut the door on the public, how then are new format ideas generated? One internal solution has been that of the think-tank, the setting up of a small group, a brains trust, inside the larger organization whose job brief is to generate and refine new concepts with a view to creating new formats. Theirs is a modern R&D laboratory whose task is not to produce scientific discoveries or come up with inventions but rather to devise TV formats. A number of companies engaged in the international television format trade have set up dedicated in-house think-tanks for the systematic creation of format concepts and ideas (C21 Media 2002).

For example, the BBC's unit for generating programme ideas and refining them is the Format Factory which is headed by the Head of Light Entertainment (World Wide Annual Review 2002). Ignition is currently the name of a comparable unit at Fremantlemedia (Flartog, Fremantlemedia 2002). Meanwhile, the Hot House is now the Entertainment Development Unit of Granada (2003). Formerly known as the Greenhouse, the unit consists of three 'ideas experts' who devised and developed more than 50 formats including *Boot Camp* (C21 Media 2002). Based in London rather than at the parent headquarters in Manchester, the unit is headed by the Creative's director of international entertainment production and formats.

All of these units exist within larger television organizations, companies that have the capacity and the need to generate format ideas that they can then take through the development stage to full television programme formats. In other words, several of this size company have production expertise and facilities such that they can develop as well as devise TV programme formats.

Nonetheless, some smaller companies restrict themselves entirely to the task of format devising. Take the case of the London-based Chatterbox Partnership (2004). The latter claims to be the United Kingdom's leading dedicated independent creator of TV formats. It is not a production company as such. Rather, it creates TV formats and licenses them to broadcasters and independent production companies. In addition, over and above what it will undertake for itself, Chatterbox also develops TV formats to order for both broadcast and non-broadcast clients. As Ben Hall, one of two founding partners of Chatterbox, put it: 'You give us an idea and we write the format for you' (Chatterbox Productions, www.ampersandcom.com /chatterbox). The company has an exclusive first look deal with Zeal television, a UK-based production and format distribution company. Half to two-thirds of Chatterbox's format catalogue has been created in-house with the rest generated from outside sources.

Generally, as a kind of research laboratory, the think-tanks display a common structure. Consisting of a small number of core full-time permanent employees or 'creatives' on contracts and producers or 'creatives' on retainers, the job of the think-tank is to devise, refine and develop intellectual property in the shape of TV programme formats. Obviously, most programme format concepts will emerge within the think-tank. However, on some occasions, ideas may also be leased or bought from outside sources, often signed to a first-look deal or contract. Hence, for example, Distraction Formats have a first-look contract with David Bodycombe, an independent UK game show format devisor. Similarly, UK Ludus has a comparable arrangement with the Australia based company, Pacific Productions.

How effective are think-tanks? Do they achieve what they were established to generate? Opinion is divided across the TV format industry as to their effectiveness or otherwise. Stephen Leahy, formerly at UK Action Time and now head of Ludus Entertainment, argues that: 'Having a load of graduates locked in a room is creatively very hard - devising a hit format is a very personal process; you have to be comfortable suggesting what might sound like a poor idea' (Hazelton 2001; C21 Media 2002; Kingsley 2003). On the other hand, those whose organizations have in-house format think-tanks obviously support this means of devising and developing format ideas.

Nonetheless, to take up Leahy's claim, just how effective are these entities? The truth probably is that while the think-tank cannot be absolutely shown to always be effective or necessary, nevertheless if the organization can afford to support such a unit, then it is probably valuable insurance in a world of uncertainty. In short, the think-tank is one means towards guaranteeing a steady supply of new format ideas which otherwise might prove to be elusive.

As example, take the following, highly revelatory story of the emergence of the format idea for Endemol's *Big Brother*:

> *Civilization might have been better served if, on that fateful evening in 1997, John de Mol had just called it a night and gone to sleep. But he couldn't stop brooding about television. It was close to midnight, at the end of a long and fruitless brainstorming session, when someone had mentioned Biosphere 2 the American media stunt that locked four men and four women in a giant glass bubble in the desert for two years. At 5 a.m. the next morning, de Mol had his inspiration, 'I was hypnotized ... I suddenly started wondering what would happen if you put a bunch of boys and girls together in a house and put them on television 24 hours a day'. He can't claim to have invented the idea; MTV's Real World was already on the air. But he milked it better.* (Anon. 2002b: 64-5)

Proponents of inspired individuals or think-tanks can both take heart from this tale. As the story is told here, de Mol may not have had the idea without the brainstorming group although the group did not actually conceive of the basic notion. In any case as the article points out, much of the necessary background for the emergence of the *Big Brother* format was already in place thanks to such earlier formats as *Real World*. Put another way, think-tanks are either vital or irrelevant to the devising of formats.

Having shed light on the matter of just who devises TV formats, the spotlight now returns to the principal subject of the format. In particular, I am interested in tracing the trail that leads from the first inspiration or impulse to create a format through to the delivery of what is called the paper format.

The format idea

In common with the business itself, I have already, several times, used the term format idea or format concept. However, it is worthwhile being clear about just what is involved here before looking at how the format process gets underway. In point of fact, the term idea is an unfortunate one. After all, an idea may be the product of a moment or a lifetime of thinking and reflection. Similarly, the term may refer to a single basic notion or to a complex set of interrelated thoughts. Additionally, as will be seen in Chapter 9, the law introduces yet another unhelpful complication by distinguishing between an idea and the expression of an idea. This latter distinction is worthy of the ancient Greek philosopher Plato, suggesting as it does, that ideas exist in some pure realm of the mind that is beyond the reach of language.

With these qualifications and distinctions in mind, one can suggest that a format idea is best thought of as an element of applied TV knowledge that can become the nucleus for the development of a TV programme format.

Clearly, and most obviously, a format idea can be seen in production and programme terms as a kind of cooking recipe from which various adaptations can be derived. The use of this analogy is very common across the television programme format industry. But, while this culinary metaphor is often a useful way of understanding what a TV programme format is, it is by no means exhaustive of the different ways of understanding the notion. Put another way, as was seen in the case of Mike Briggs and *Who Wants to be a Millionaire?* an idea may be vague as such. It may, too, not be the kernel or seed of a programme on air but rather be a way of doing business, a marketing notion, a means of setting up a kind of golden goose so far as programme production, profit sources, spin-offs and so on is concerned. Hence, as demonstrated by the example of *Romper Room* cited in the previous chapter, the core of a format idea may lie in the recognition of a particular income stream or merchandising opportunity. Equally, with the startup of TV soap opera format adaptations such as *Goede Tijden, Slechte Tijden* (*The Restless Years*) and *Joy Luck Street* (*Coronation Street*) in the Netherlands and the Peoples' Republic of China, respectively, it was not the dramatic narratives and characters of the originals that were at stake in format licensing (Moran 2000; Moran & Keane 2005). Rather, in both instances, it was the complex set of production knowledges having to do with the establishment of writing and production teams, storylining, work routines and schedules, resource allocation and general production organization that lay at the heart of these adaptations. In other words, one impulse towards a format arrangement may look and may be very different to another. To subsume these different motivations and knowledges under the blanket term of format concept or idea creates unnecessary confusion and obfuscation.

Identifying a format idea

How, then, do creatives go about devising a format? Where is the knowledge for a format idea to be found? The obvious answer is that creating a new TV format concept does not take place in a vacuum. After all, the devisor will be thinking television so that television must be the material that he or she is working with. For the most part, devising does not appear to be the craft of conjuring something out of thin air. Instead, it seems more appropriate to think of a format concept as the genie locked up in the magic bottle. What the devisor is trying to do is to release or unlock this format idea, the nucleus of intelligence around which other knowledges can then begin to form and crystallize.

So TV homework is essential. Put another way, the devisor needs to be right up to date, if not already ahead of the game, with what is happening everywhere in television industries in general and with the format business in particular. Obviously, money is a key factor here so far as this kind of international coverage is concerned. The larger companies in broadcasting, format development and production can apply more resources to the job of gathering up-to-date information about just what is currently happening. Recall, for instance, the creation of Endemol's GCT mentioned in Chapter 1. In a nutshell, the more resources you have, the more up to date your intelligence and information is and the fresher your format idea is likely to be.

But even where finance is restricted, as in the case of the independent or would-be devisor, there is still much that can be done with native wit and raw intelligence. For example, it goes without saying that the 'creative' will watch as much television as possible. In addition, industry insiders also suggest that it is useful and even necessary to read as much as possible about what is happening in different TV industries in as many places as possible. Various on-line services and magazines help provide this information. Several of these sources are listed in Appendix i. Frequent visits to the websites of networks in different places to access programme guides and related material are also seen as vital for a would-be devisor. On-the-ground links in other places are important. Hence, for example, Australian game show wizard Reg Grundy is reported to have first come across the format of *Man O Man* on a German cable station while turning the TV satellite dial on his yacht in the Mediterranean (Brooke 1995).

David Bodycombe, game show specialist, who has helped in the devising and development of *The Mole* (Channel 5), *Sub Zero* (BBC2), and *The Crystal Maze* (Channel 4), suggests that it is also useful to know about the past history of the particular programme genre in which the format is being devised (see Appendix ii). Such knowledge may alert a devisor to other format possibilities.

In any case, he recommends an active programme watching, by a would-be devisor with an eye to attempting to work out a programme's inner 'rules' - the way that budget, resources, work routines, and so on help shape it. In other words, the newcomer or would-be devisor should try to think through what makes a particular programme distinctive. To help with this programme format homework, Bodycombe pinpoints a number of elements to be examined. These include:

- Identifying a programme's parts
- The connections between the parts
- The differences between episodes
- Principal on-screen figures
- Timeslot and scheduling choices
- The programme's intended audience

Drafting and refining

However, this kind of homework is one thing. Actually getting started is another. According to the various industry personnel that I spoke to, getting the nub of a format knowledge down on paper is where the process really begins. Therefore, a first draft stage in developing even a paper format involves a short, written outline of the programme idea and its key rules. This might contain several original and unique notions which are frequently, nowadays, described as engines (Adair & Moran 2004: 24-8). Hence, with a format such as that of *Who Wants to be a Millionaire?*, these engines included having a major prize of a million pound or dollars, giving contestants a set of possible answers, offering a series of 'lifelines', using a host with a supercilious manner and soundtrack and lighting to dramatic effect.

Altogether, the short outline of the initial format idea might run to no more than 100 words, a paragraph or so, perhaps in point form. Probably, too, this will be written up by one person, working alone or in a small team. Like the most rudimentary of maps, this overview stakes out the broad landscape of the programme concept. Such an outline represents the basic pitch of the format idea. It can also serve as pretext to engage the creative and even the business involvement of others.

Julie Christie of Touchdown Productions, formerly based in New Zealand but now relocated to the United States, explained this step as follows:

> *We [she and her production partner] will talk about the idea - sometimes for as little as about half an hour. Then I will attempt to write up the format. That first bit will be about one page - in fact one paragraph. If you cannot say it in one paragraph, then you cannot say it at all.* (Interview Moran 2003)

Subsequently, further work occurs with this initial written idea. In particular, devisors deliberately identify various 'rules' (or 'engines') in the documentation of the idea. Again, Julie Christie, saw these as various 'triggers' for a format, restrictions that could liberate certain possibilities in the programme:

> *The 'rules' of a format are the triggers that free up certain behaviour, or influence certain behaviour of the participants. Like, for example,* Changing Rooms. *It all has to be done in 48 hours. It triggers a rush. The fact that you have only $500. It triggers innovation and being smart with money.* (Interview Moran 2003)

Each stage of this devising-related thinking is documented so that the initial written idea is continually being updated and redrafted. Obviously, the paper record or document that summarizes all of this is growing in length although it still runs to no more than two or three pages. However, once something is down on paper and starting to grow in detail, there is an opportunity to begin refining it.

In other words, even as the single devisor or the devising team put together the format idea, the programme concept, it is also necessary to simultaneously dismantle it. The object is to have a harder, more critical look at the originating notion. Experienced industry professionals believe that the general advice at this stage should be to run through the detailed concept again and again and again, as often as time will allow and patience will endure. The aim, they suggest, is to identify the format idea's weaknesses and faults as part of the process of refining and improving the draft format.

Again, Bodycomb in his advice for would-be devisors offers a very useful list of practical considerations for helping to screen the emerging format idea (Appendix ii). These include matters of finance and revenue to do with production budget and income streams, issues of schedule and resources, considerations of safety and insurance, production practicalities and even matters of entertainment value. However, his checklist is aimed at the novice or newcomer devisor who is forced to work alone. While being part of a team of some kind does not banish these considerations, it does all the same (as will be seen in the next section) - assist in answering some of the more practical matters in a more organized way.

Working collaboratively

Put another way, it is always better to be in touch with others as a means of strengthening and expanding a format. For while there are examples of successful 'lone wolf' devisors, such as John Lewis cited above, nevertheless, some kind of collaboration would seem to be essential. This is the case not least because individuals are often not in the best position to grasp all the strengths and weaknesses in their own ideas.

Even one other experienced person can be an effective sounding board. Mark Overett who co-devised the game show *In The Dark* put it this way:

> In The Dark *was a collective at different stages of having a variety of voices talking it through. I think once you've got the experience though your guts tell you when its right and wrong and, your right, you only need the sounding board of one person, so long as it is a person whose opinion you value and you know they are either going to tell you its crap or its great.* (Interview Moran 2002)

Usually, though, a sounding board is more than one person. Casting the entire office staff in such a role is common in TV programme format companies. Julie Christy explained more about this particular stage and tactic:

> We will get in a bunch of producers from here and start to pitch it to them to see what weaknesses they pick up. We are in effect trialling it. We will look at the format and go 'what are the worst things about that format?' Or say, 'how would we make that if we had an endless budget. A bottomless pit of money - how would we make this. So we look at the extremes and often they trigger something in your mind. It's hard to explain. It's like anti-brainstorming.' It's 'what's really bad about this format'. Instead of looking at what's good. That often provokes other ideas in your mind. (Interview Moran 2003)

However, Christie is talking about a company where such experience is readily available to be tapped in this way. What about the situation of an individual devisor, a John Lewis or a Fintan Coyle, who can come up with initial ideas but is not, necessarily, in a position to take the fledgling format much further. As has already been seen, these two outsiders approached Channel 4 and the BBC respectively and those organizations then put them into contact with experienced producers in order to develop their ideas.

At one level, though, times appear to have changed. For budget reasons but also because of possible legal action in the future, many companies that, hitherto, would read uninvited format ideas, are no longer prepared to do so.

Nevertheless, there does seem to be a perennial number of small, often new companies that are willing to read written format ideas and work with newcomers to help develop these into paper formats that can be taken to a broadcaster and are ready for commissioning for pilot production. Dublin-based Midas and London-based Playback are two such entities - small companies who have the necessary devising and production experience to refine initial paper concepts. Additionally, this kind of company will and must have credibility, a track-record with broadcasters such that some of its personnel will then double-up in producer and director roles in subsequent pilot production. Put another way, the place in the system of this kind of company is to function in the gap between concept and paper format, taking format ideas forward towards development.

Finally, then, before leaving the subject of devising, it is also worth mentioning the view from the other side. As is explained in the next chapter, devisors - especially if they are newcomers - need experienced producers and production companies to help them in the development and commissioning of their format ideas. Hence, Bob Campbell, head of Screentime, told of that company's interaction with creatives:

> *We see everyone who wants to see us. We make it a policy of seeing everyone some of whom have the most outrageous ideas you have ever seen or heard. Some of whom have good ideas but no idea of how to realize them. And some people have very well developed ideas and substantial reputations who need us to go and draw the threads together and get a commission from an investor.* (Interview Moran 2003)

In summary then, devising is only the first stage in the journey towards the realization of a fully matured programme format. Although the activity is - as has been suggested - typically surrounded with notions of originality and individual innovation - yet much of it can be seen as restricted or negotiated creativity, routinized inspiration within the general field of television. In any case, devising is seen to be a labour not fully formed in itself but rather one that is intimately dependent on a further process of gestation. Accordingly, I now move on to the next stage of the TV programme format-making process, taking up the story of development in the next chapter.

CHAPTER 4

Format development

Paper formats ... are initially a viability study of the idea and often a selling tool. They contain the first set of ingredients on which the final format recipe is based. They are the catalysts around which all the resources that go into producing a television programme first start to gather.

John Gough, Distraction (Bodycombe 2002)

Production companies get you to a network. Creators cannot get there.

David Franken, Former network programming manager (Adair & Moran 2004)

The golden rule as an independent is try not to pay for anything yourself.

Mark Overett, Format Producer (Adair & Moran 2004)

The paper format

As suggested, format creation is the process whereby a programme idea is increasingly and more fully articulated by the devisor both to herself/himself and to others. Hence, in the stage formally known as devising, an initial format idea or concept is written out, thought through, even submitted to some imaginative trialling and testing, perhaps among a small group of professionals or friends or both. In turn, this initial phase of format making gives way to another known as that of development. This witnesses the writing up of a fuller outline than that involved in the initial paper draft. This second, more inclusive document is called the paper format (sometimes - quite confusingly - abbreviated to just the format).

As I suggested in Chapter 2, programme adaptation and licensing in broadcasting has been going on for at least 50 years. However, what is relatively novel and recent is the concern with document drafting, including the preparation of a paper format, as part of a process of creating a readily adaptable format. Hence, it is now customary to expand in written form on the background concept with the result being labelled as the paper format. This documentation encompasses the detailed interlocking format knowledges from stage set and layout to commercial and budgetary considerations.

The advent of this kind of written entity represents a considerable change within broadcasting business. Less than fifteen years ago it was fairly unusual for a format idea to be systematically committed to paper in this kind of way. This is not of course to deny that various thoughts, information, instructions and so on were not written down. But the point of the change is that such entities as the paper format are instruction kits for the future rather than for the present. A paper format and a written format Bible were highly unusual in the past. Instead, the awareness of a pre-existing plan or recipe that gave rise to a programme could, mostly, only be inferred once the actual programme first went to air. And even then, the full set of codified elements may not have been spelled out on paper or available in tangible and accessible form. Those who wished to copy or adapt the format had to deduce a good deal of its content and its logics from what could be seen when it was broadcast.

The paper format usually runs to several pages in length. One devisor mentioned five or six while another suggested as many as ten. Such a document will contain both the programme idea and the successive rules or logics that organize its action. This action is not restricted to production but can cover a range of other areas including finance, marketing, broadcasting and cross platforming. Again, these are elements that can only be dimly perceived (if at all) from a broadcast programme. Nevertheless, how a programme 'works' for producers, for participants both on and off screen, and for the audience often commands initial attention in the paper format. Thus, for example, if the planning of a programme format for a game show is to involve three games, then the paper format might comprise a brief outline of its different elements. These could include an explanation of how each of these games work; how the score operates; how contestants are eliminated; an outline of the prizes and how these function; the style of the host's activity, appearance and dialogue; and how the host's role works. All of this is made clearer in a written outline. This document is the paper format.

So, what does a paper format look like? Again, there are no hard and fast rules, but a very detailed description would give most of the information necessary to make a programme starting from scratch. Usually the document runs to less than ten pages of A4 paper in length. Additionally, a website for new devisors warns that the paper format should not appear intimidating to read (www.tvformats.com). The same site suggests that it should be neatly printed by a word processor. On the other hand, among more experienced personnel in the business, some paper formats have been accepted on a scrappy piece of typewriter paper, and even during a lunch conversation.

More specifically, this document may contain some or all of the following knowledge elements:

- Programme title
- Target audience
- Suggested timeslot
- Length (in minutes)
- Brief outline (two to three sentences)
- Outline running order
- Round structure (if applicable)
- Detailed synopsis
- Sample games/questions
- Illustrations
- Suggested presenters
- Budget overview
- Set design

- Merchandising opportunities
- Suggestions about other income streams

In fact, within the general category of the paper format, the industry is increasingly differentiating between two forms of the document. Briefly, what has been outlined so far makes up the 'long-form' of the paper format. This is the fuller, more expanded and inclusive version of the document. On the other hand, there is also the 'short-form', a more abbreviated, summary version of the same thing. The latter is not to be confused with the initial written or scribbled format idea which occurs at the beginning of the devising process. By contrast, getting ready the 'short-form' version of the paper format occurs later, usually after the extended version has been prepared.

Nonetheless, the 'short-form' is intended to sit next to the 'long-form' version, one offering the full outline while the other provides a bare bone summary. Running in length between a paragraph and one or two pages, the elements of the 'short-form' paper format will be few, perhaps including:

- Programme title
- General principle or premise of the programme
- Target audience
- Suggested host
- A few sentences outlining the main stages

Obviously, the initial jotting of the format idea may be of some use here in preparing this latter summary. In any case, it is usually necessary to go through the process of writing the 'long-form' version which is then condensed down into this form. The purpose of this particular document is clear. Like the blurb on a CD, video or book, the 'short-form' paper format works both to give a brief overview of what the programme format will include and to arouse further interest from broadcasters and production companies.

These levels of detail in the paper format, especially in the 'long-form', are important because the format idea is now going public. Even though the process of drafting and refining outlined in the last chapter has, frequently, involved the use of outsiders with production experience, nevertheless, the process of devising is, mostly, a private fairly individual affair. But, once the format idea has been filled out and refined in the shape of the paper format, it is necessary and timely to approach a broadcaster or a producer both to test levels of interest and to secure necessary finance for further work.

In this situation, the level of detail contained in a paper format is important for the devisor both in terms of pitching the format idea to a would-be producer or broadcaster and as a means of attempting to secure some legal protection of the property. Within the bounds of this model, the paper format helps the broadcaster or producer gain a better sense of what is original and unique about a particular programme idea. Hence, the paper format also functions as a lever towards a commissioning. Secondly, a written outline is necessary because producers and broadcasters are cautious to the point of refusing to listen to new programme ideas pitched to them, especially, where these have not been committed to paper. Third, on the creator or devisor's part, documentation of authorship of the original work and all revisions with the relevant dates is essential should later disagreement or dispute arise between parties. Experienced format devisors and developers also see it as a smart move to supplement the paper format with other forms of documentation such as photographs, drawings and even some moving images. After all, as I will explain later, there is no such thing as a single format right although, paradoxically, format 'rights' are licensed as well as being bought and sold each week for large sums of money.

By way of example, one can cite a paper format prepared in connection with a would be game show entitled *Don't Blow a Fuse!* (This later evolved into *In The Dark!* - see Chapter 5). The (paper) format runs to six A4 pages. Its cover announces it as a 'Format' with a draft date in 1995, identification and a copyright claim in the names of John Gough, Mark Overett and Colin Skevington. The page also contains the briefest of summaries - '1. Three couples take up amusing challenges in the dark (and light) to win watts ... ever mindful of not blowing a fuse! 2. The winning couple convert their watts to light to find fuses that light up prizes'. In turn, the succeeding five pages set out a kind of script or running order for an episode of the programme in a series of short paragraphs. Each paragraph sets out in summary form the activity of host or contestants or the point in the succession of games, adverts and so on.

Agents and partners

Before looking to the pitching or submission to a broadcaster of a production proposal (in the shape of this kind of paper format), it is worth noting that depending on the size of the broadcasting market, then intermediaries may need to be brought into the picture. Indeed, go-betweens of one sort or another are a recurring feature of the business at all stages and at very many levels. I have, for example, already noticed the existence of small devising and development companies such as Midas and Playback that can help turn a format idea into a paper format. Having a collaboration with companies known to broadcasters might be a necessary step in getting to pitch a would-be format to a broadcaster.

Such companies needn't only be at the smaller end of the scale. As well as devising their own formats, larger companies also frequently act as mentors for much smaller companies that have no track record and are not recognized by broadcasters. Obviously, the latter are not prepared to trust them with production commissions and, indeed, are unwilling to deal with them at all. Hence, by getting into a relationship with the larger company, the small, relatively unknown company, comes, in part, to acquire not only a partner but also a kind of joint agent to deal with the broadcaster.

Similarly, in very large markets such as that of the United States, it is only agents acting on behalf of a devisor who are in position to approach a broadcaster. Indeed, agents are very important in facilitating movement in this industry, constantly acting as gatekeepers with two different kinds of interests, above as well as below, to satisfy. We shall return to their crucial role in format distribution in the next chapter.

Development collaborations

The next step in the enlargement of the format is that of development. In many territories, the paper format devisor now sets about approaching and pitching the format to a producer or broadcaster. There are several reasons for the latter's involvement from this stage onwards. For one thing, investing in the development of what looks like a potentially successful programme idea is a way of ensuring that that group has first option on the final programme format. Additionally, such an involvement also helps to guarantee that the interests, needs and wishes of the broadcaster are being taken into account. As Geoff Stevens of TVNZ put it:

> As a baseline, new producers wanting to build a relationship with TVNZ must look at what's currently screening, what's working and what's not, note which companies are making which kinds of successful programmes and decide which programmes you respect and like in terms of production values, ideas, energy, qualities. The best thing you can then do is approach the production companies who you think can best deliver your programme and form a relationship with them. There are virtually no 'musthave' ideas out there, the programmes that get to the screen result from a close relationship between the commissioner and the producer. (Interview Moran 2003)

Despite this, there is at least one other way to achieve the same result, namely the involvement of a producer or broadcaster who will finance the further development of the format, including, perhaps, the videotaping of a programme pilot. This alternative route is that of the show-reel. Julie Christy of Touchdown Productions regularly makes show-reels to highlight programme formats in development. The show-reel is in effect a commercial for the format idea, a kind of video presentation or pitch to a would-be producer or investor.

Running about 30 seconds in length, it will involve some video recording as well as various computer generated material integrated together so as to constitute an advertisement for the format. It is produced with potential production investors in mind such as those encountered at the format trade fairs.

Frequently put together early in the cycle, even while the paper format is being developed, the show-reel will contain only general information about the uniqueness of the concept. This comes about not only because the paper format is still in development but also because of the need at this stage to avoid saying too much publicly about the format idea.

So, whether an investor is found through pitching only the paper format or else by also seeing a show-reel, nevertheless, the outcome is the same. More investment means that further development work can occur on the format concept. Typically, this might mean extended fleshing out of the idea in a lot more detail by drawing on the services of other production people or even proceeding to make a pilot based on the paper format. Clearly, the latter marks a new stage in the development of the programme format.

Trialling

Obviously, it is highly relevant to rehearse or road test the format idea as it has been progressively refined. Undoubtedly, though, some formats such as those to do with 'reality' programmes might be difficult to simulate. On the other hand, game show formats are among the easiest to run-through and trial. Here, a well-trodden path is to have family, friends and others play the various onscreen parts in live walk-through games or rounds, much like a kind of group reading of a new stage play both as a means of its further development and also as a means of persuading larger theatrical interests to become financially and artistically involved in this process. However, with the TV programme format development, it is also, probably, possible to simulate other segments of other format ideas such as that to do with comedy, cooking, home improvement and magazine items.

At this stage, the intention is threefold. First, to refine the full idea or even a part by staging it. Those developing the format need to ask themselves just how clear in practice are the format's rules so far as both the participants and would-be viewers are concerned. How efficient and effective are the various parts of the format when put through their paces? A 'dress rehearsal' is a very useful way to show a would-be investor such as a broadcaster just how a format works.

Clearly, too, no matter how often those developing the format have run through it by way of brainstorming, devil's advocate and office discussion, a dry run of this sort is also an important opportunity to grasp just how it works. Focussing on game show formats, Bodycombe suggests:

Get some of your friends to play an improvised mockup of the game. Take note of how long it takes them to understand the rules. Does the strategy of the game reward contestants that take risks and play offensively rather than defensive, sandbagging play? A programme might be fun to play, but is it going to be interesting to the viewers? In particular, is there a 'playalong' factor - that is, can the viewers try to answer the questions, games or puzzles before the contestants do? (2002)

The pilot

This kind of rehearsal or simulation is one way to further test and expand a format. Equally, though, there is also what is referred to as the pilot. A long established practice in the television production industry, the pilot refers to the making of a sample episode as a kind of down payment on a series. For the producer, a pilot is an opportunity to put on screen what has, so far, existed only on paper. More importantly, for the commissioning broadcaster, the pilot is a sample of the full series and so offers a further means of ensuring that the expense involved in committing to a series of programmes is financially justified (Alesandro 1997).

In turn, two kinds of pilots have become associated with format development. The first and more familiar kind is what might be called the studio pilot. This is a kind of full dress rehearsal for the real thing and involves the use of all resources that would come into play in an actual production including studio, professional crew and performers, recording, editing and so on. On the other hand, there is a more modestly budgeted and more improvised pilot which is frequently called the office pilot. This is a workshop pilot or run-through, filmed with a domestic video camera in the production office of the development company, with secretaries and other employees, family and friends acting as contestants, host, audience and so on.

Unless there is a particular reason to go for a more professional pilot shot in a television studio with its attendant increase in costs, format developers are tending to favour this more modest form of filmed run-through as the next step in the development chain.

In any case, like all pilot episodes, the overall intention is clear: to test how well the format works with cast and crew playing before camera and audience. This kind of modest piloting can also serve incidental purposes such as allowing the trialling of other material and performers. More particularly, though, the video recording becomes useful for reference purposes. It contributes to the ongoing documentation of the format. Additionally, together with the paper format, it helps to flesh out and visualize the format concept. Ben Silverman, formerly an agent with the UK branch of the William Morris agency, expanded on this point:

> *The notion that you're buying into something that has actually been produced and that preexists makes it a much more valuable enterprise for a network buyer, because they are seeing something that they can look at. 'Oh, that's what happens when the sand gets thrown on the girl's face.' 'Oh, that's where you go when you introduce the gay boyfriend into the scene.'* (Goldsmith 2001)

The role-playing and recording also offers an opportunity to bring in a broadcaster for an informal and private preview. The latter's advice and suggestions can also feed back into the thinking of the format developers. Mark Overett offered an illustration of how helpful a run through before cameras could be in persuading others to back a format idea:

> *One of the ways we got* In The Dark *up to get a pilot, how John [Gough] and I got Uharai and Fuji on board. We hired a small studio at LWT and actually ... that was the second one, the first one we just hired a little private studio, and we lit it and put out our PBS cameras in there and it was pokey dark. And we created an obstacle course in the dark and we put little glow in the dark stickers on the floor that was an S shape and around it we put, not a Ming Vase, but giant vases and a table with champagne glass pyramids on top of them. And basically we took Mr Uharai in and said follow the line, we are meeting at the end of the line. So then we walked the line and we turned the lights up and he had just seen what he had walked through to get to us. And then we played the tape back and he went - 'Oh, I understand the show now'. So that's how we sort of got people involved.* (Interview Moran 2002)

Hence, the pilot may be a means of selling a format to a producer. It also functions as an opportunity for spotting and resolving problems on the part of the format developer.

In the field of format distribution, a pilot, whether undertaken in an office or in a studio, also serves another related function. In effect, the pilot becomes part of the package of services and knowledge for a would-be adapter of the format. A recording, whether undertaken in the office or in a television studio, helps to further define and concretize a format as it is explained and illustrated in the paper format. The pilot can substitute in a programme format package for an off-air episode until the first programme based on the format is broadcast. Once this happens, then a broadcast recording becomes available for inclusion in the package, offering an actual example of how a format concept was visualized on air.

It is worth adding here that, in practice, it is common for formats to give rise to more than one pilot of either type. After all, a pilot is seen in the industry as a relatively inexpensive way of ensuring that the cost of a series is or is not justified. While some paper formats are seen not to require pilots before production goes ahead, others have been known to have been piloted more than half a dozen times. Indeed, as already noted, development can take a considerable amount of time with the multiple production of pilots becoming common.

Finally, too, I mentioned above about beginning to go public with a format. Even becoming involved with a development team increases the number of people who are aware of the format idea. Once this has been written up as a paper format, then it is useful and necessary to begin to publicize what is being developed. Even early disclosure of a programme title and a brief outline can help lay claim to the format idea. Of course, it is also a way of suggesting to others that they should not trespass on this territory. Once further development work has occurred and there is interest from a broadcaster, then the format devisor and producer will begin to release even more details to the media about the format. As has already been suggested, TV programme ideas are frequently 'in the air' so that going public in this way can help to safeguard a particular format idea.

Format production and the broadcast programme

This account of the development of a format now moves forward to production and broadcast. Broadcasters often prefer to produce programmes based on formats in-house because they believe that this enables them to control costs. In this case, a licensor will insist that the development group has a set of attachments to the production. Attachment clauses might specify that the production should engage various of their personnel in such capacities as producer and director.

By this stage too, if not earlier, a devisor who has little or no experience in TV production will have to let go of the format idea that s/he originated. On the other hand, a new devisor may also, for whatever reason, be in a position to insist on producing or co-producing the format as a broadcast programme. In such a case, like those in the development team, this person derives income from both the format licensing and from the production.

Equally often, though, broadcasters may simply contract the production company involved in the format's development to produce the first adaptation on its behalf. Again, the principles of the latter will now gain revenue from their involvement in such roles as that of producer and director.

Most of the time, the intellectual property connected with a format remains with the creator/producer, even if the broadcaster fully-funds the show. However, there are exceptions. On other occasions, these might be shared with the broadcaster who has invested in the first production. Hence, devisor, development team and broadcaster now stand to generate revenues from the formats distribution in other markets.

Drawing attention to these production arrangements is important. They serve here to prevent us picking up the mistaken impression that copyright in written documents is paramount for devisors. Rather, what is practically important is the revenue streams derived from a programme including its production. Hence, while a devisor may take copyright in a written format, the production company will take a copyright in the programme itself. Again, for example, while a third to a half of UK Chatterbox's formats have been devised outside the company, nonetheless, the company increases its financial stake in these by writing all programmes based on them.

The evolution of a format: *Who Wants to be a Millionaire?*

To complete this discussion of the devising and development of a format, one can turn to an account of the evolution of this British game show. Although the programme's background has already been touched upon, nonetheless the following account serves to highlight the often torturous processes involved in these particular stages as well as the combination of circumstances that led finally to its first broadcast. It should also be noted that the account is not uncontested by others who alleged in a series of legal actions that the format owed something to other formats although this was not a view shared by Celador, the owner of the format (England High Court 2004).

The origin of *Who Wants to be a Millionaire?* was a programme proposal devised by David Briggs in 1995. From 1972 to 1994, he had worked at UK's Capital Radio in a number of senior positions including Head of Competitions and Executive Producer of the *Chris Tarrant Show*. In some of these positions Briggs was responsible for deciding upon the use of, and in some cases devising, competitions, the majority of which were phone in competitions in which contestants won prizes by answering a series of questions. From 1984 to 1988 his colleagues included Michael Whitehill and Steven Knight. From 1994 to 1996 he was Head of Marketing at GMTV, where he had responsibility for promoting competitions many of which included the use of premium rate telephone lines to answer multiple-choice quizzes.

Briggs' proposal was for a quiz programme entitled *The Cash Mountain* in which contestants would answer multiple-choice questions the value of which doubled with each question. After each round the contestants would have the choice of leaving the game and keeping the money they had won or staying in, with the risk that they would lose their winnings if they gave a wrong answer. The prize money was to be substantially funded by revenue from calls on premium lines from prospective contestants seeking to enter the quiz. He saw the programme as a vehicle for Chris Tarrant.

In early autumn 1995 Briggs had lunch with Whitehill. He described his proposal to the latter who suggested that he put the proposal in writing and send it to Paul Smith, the Chief Executive of Celador. Celador was and is a well-known UK independent television production company. Since 1988, Whitehill and Knight had been contracted to provide writing and other creative services to Celador, and they had worked on numerous projects including devising and developing three game shows. They shared an office at Celador's premises and saw Smith regularly.

In October 1995 Briggs produced a written proposal for *The Cash Mountain* dated 23 October 1995 ('*Cash Mountain* Version 1') that he sent to Whitehill. The latter showed this to Paul Smith, who was enthusiastic but considered that the proposal needed development. The document comprised five typed pages. The proposal involved five essential features, namely:

1. Contestants were to be selected by correctly answering six questions over the telephone in a call by the contestant on a premium line.

2. The prizes would be funded by the revenue to be derived from the use of the premium line.

3. In the course of the programme a number of contestants would be asked a series of multiple-choice questions. A correct answer would entitle the contestant to a money prize. Each successive prize would be double that of the earlier one but if the contestant gave a wrong answer then all previous prizes were lost.

4. About two thirds of the way through the programme the contestant who was then in the lead would go into 'the sweatbox' and play on alone for the highest value prizes.

5. There were to be three optional prize structures for twenty questions. In the first option the prizes ran from £10 for question one to £5,242,880 for question twenty. The range for the second and third options were respectively £25 and £13,107,200 and £100 and £52,428,800.

During the period from November 1995 to January/February 1996 the proposal was developed by Whitehill, Knight and Smith with occasional input from Briggs. During this period the former trio came up with the ideas of having 21 questions leading to a top prize of £1m, allowing contestants to view questions before deciding whether to answer them, providing contestants with a guaranteed level of prize money if they answered a certain number of questions correctly (safe havens) and allowing contestants three forms of assistance ('helping hands' later known as 'lifelines'). Whitehill came up with the idea for the 'Ask the Audience' lifeline, Mr Knight came up the idea for the 'Phone a Friend' lifeline and one of the three came up with the idea for the '50/50' lifeline. Various other ideas for lifelines were canvassed and rejected. At the end of this process Michael Whitehill produced a revised written proposal entitled *Cash Mountain* ('*Cash Mountain* Version 2'). This is an eight page typed document. The first page is a cover sheet which specifies *Cash Mountain* as a series of 13 x 45 minute programmes and bears the legend '(c) Celador Productions Ltd 1996'.

On or around 20 February 1996 Paul Smith 'pitched' the *Cash Mountain* proposal to Claudia Rosencrantz, Controller of Network Entertainment at ITV Network Ltd. Ms Rosencrantz was very enthusiastic, although she had reservations about certain aspects of the proposal including the title. The two agreed that Tarrant would be the perfect host for the proposed programme. Rosencrantz suggested that Smith should 'pitch' the proposal to Marcus Plantin, the then

Figure 4.1 Eddie McGuire in Australia's *Who Wants to be a Millionaire?*

Director of Programmes, whose authorization was required before a programme could be commissioned. On 27 February 1996 he 'pitched' the proposal to Plantin. *Cash Mountain* was logged in ITV's proposal log on the same day. The Director was not willing to commission the programme, but did agree to commission some qualitative market research to gauge likely audience reaction.

This research was carried out by The Qualitative Consultancy in July 1996. In August 1996 the agency delivered a report to ITV which was positive about the programme's potential and made suggestions regarding a number of its features including noting that reaction to the title *Cash Mountain* was very negative, that the word 'million' was considered the key word to communicate the concept and create appeal and that alternative titles suggested included 'To be a Millionaire'. Nevertheless on 6 September 1996 Rosencrantz wrote to Smith to say that ITV would not commission the programme.

Subsequently he offered the proposal to Channel 5, Channel 4, Sky, LWT and Carlton. All expressed interest, but none commissioned the programme. In November 1996 he tried again to persuade Plantin to commission the proposal, but without success. In July 1997 Rosencrantz was requested by Smith to reconsider the idea.

However, the fate of the format was about to change. In September 1997 David Liddiment replaced Marcus Plantin as ITV's Director of Programmes. Ms Rosencrantz recommended to Mr Liddiment that ITV should commission *Cash Mountain* with Chris Tarrant as a possible host. On 22 October 1997 Michael Smith wrote to Mr Liddiment enclosing a revised proposal ('*Cash Mountain* Version 3') and asking for fifteen minutes to discuss it with him. *Cash Mountain* Version 3 comprises a cover sheet and five typed pages. The cover sheet bears the legend '(c) Celador Productions Ltd 1997'. The body of the document contains a description of the original proposal as modified in the subsequent discussions. It incorporated into *Cash Mountain* Version 2 various aspects suggested by the Qualitative Consultancy Report, including the number of questions, the maximum prize of £1m., the omission of musical acts and the method of selecting contestants.

On 5 December 1997, Liddiment met him and effectively agreed to commission the programme, although formal commissioning did not take place until around 24 April 1988. The new Director suggested that the programme should be 'stripped' (broadcast sequentially) over consecutive nights. Chris Tarrant was still the favoured presenter.

In January 1998, Celador produced a revised proposal (*Cash Mountain* Version 4) incorporating Liddiment's suggestion that the programme be 'stripped' over consecutive nights. In addition the contestant recruitment process was changed from one involving radio stations to a process in which potential contestants had to phone a premium line and answer three questions correctly to be entered into a pool from which ten would be randomly selected for each programme. At the beginning of the programme these ten would be asked a question and the one who keyed in the correct answer first would qualify as the first contestant ('fastest finger first'). *Cash Mountain* Version 4 is a copy of *Cash Mountain* Version 3, the alterations being incorporated by amendments to the fourth page.

ITV now asked Celador to devise an alternative title. In March 1988 Celador produced lists of possible alternative titles devised by Briggs, Whitehill and Knight. One of the alternative titles, which was suggested by Whitehill, was *Who Wants to be a Millionaire?*, after the Cole Porter song of the same name which was featured in the film *High Society*. From these lists Ms Rosencrantz selected the title *Who Wants to be a Millionaire?* in late March/early April 1998.

Lists of possible presenters were also produced in March 1988. In May 1988 Chris Tarrant was selected as the presenter. Paul Smith suggested that he should wear dark clothing. Around May 1998 the prize structure was changed so as to reduce the number of questions to fifteen ranging in prize money from £1 to £1m. The set was devised by Andy Walmsley during the period May to September 1998 in accordance with a brief from Smith. The latter also suggested that the host and contestant should sit on high stools.

A pilot programme was recorded on 17 August 1998. Mike Briggs acted as associate producer on the pilot, assisting and coaching Chris Tarrant. Whitehill and Knight were also involved in developing links for the presenter. Following the pilot programme Ms Rosencrantz suggested that the prize structure for the first five questions be changed so as to start at £100 and that there should be a box of money on stage. Smith came up with the idea of Tarrant handing over cheques to the contestants on stage and tearing up earlier cheques. He also commissioned new music from Keith Strachan to replace music by Peter Waterman (commissioned for the pilot) which Rosencrantz considered unsatisfactory. Celador also decided to change the expression 'helping hands' to 'lifelines'. The first episode of *Who Wants to be a Millionaire?* was transmitted on 4 September 1998.

Altogether, this story is highly instructive about the complicated process of negotiation that occurs in the devising and development stages of the evolution of a TV format. Typically, many were involved, hardly surprising given the large number of elements in a programme. At the same time, as the story is told here, it is also clear that an emerging format encounters a series of organizational gatekeepers at different levels of a television institution and their decisions affect whether or not the process of development goes forward or is stalled. Finally, too, it is also worth noting the succession of documentations of the paper format that are recorded. Clearly, these were important stages in the evolution of the format and would, of course, turn out to be vital for Celador's case in the High Court against a number of claimants.

However, be this as it may, the story of a format's evolution does not halt with the programme's first broadcast. Instead, distribution of the format to other producers in other territories is a further crucial component of the chain. In other words, for the sake of this discussion, the circulation mechanism that is distribution now becomes the driving force in the further elaboration of the format. In other circumstances, such as that outlined in Figure 3.1 above, the broadcasting of a programme would, usually, be the end of the story of its development. At such a point - the on-air broadcast - the making of a television programme is, normally, complete and that completion is registered both in the fact that the show has been put to air and is also shortly to be offered for licensed broadcast in other territories. For a TV programme format, on the other hand, its first broadcast, while very important in the chain of the format's elaboration, is only incidental in the development of the knowledges that can be provided to a licensed adapter elsewhere. Put another way, the information and insight generated by the programme broadcast becomes another element that is included in the format package. Hence, the account now proceeds to examine a further and final stage in the format's elaboration which occurs as part of the process of distribution. This stage is the subject of the next chapter.

CHAPTER 5

Distributing formats

I prefer to describe what I do as a miner for high end intellectual property. The fact that it manifests itself in the dimension of television tends to add the kitsch value to it immediately. But we have been involved in brokering the deals for Big Brother, The Weakest Link, Dog Eat Dog, Who Wants to be a Millionaire? *etc.*

Ben Silverman formerly with William Morris UK (Hazelton 2000)

Minimize the risks - formats offer tried and tested creative ideas for reliable quality programming. Grasp the essentials - each package contains many elements you need to make an individual series tailor-made to your own particular requirements.

BBC WorldWide Format Guide blurb (2003)

As a format devisor you've got to decide at the end of the day what business you're in. What's your primary business? Is your primary business devising formats? Is your primary business distributing? That's another point. Also as a format devisor you've got to make a decision about when you let go.

Mark Overett (Adair & Moran 2004)

TV programme format distribution is primarily about franchising not TV programming. This is not to say that the past success of a particular programme is not an important springboard in the exchange between format devisor/owner and licensee. Actually, it is crucial. However, its importance lies in the fact that the programme's previous ratings success is the attraction that leads to a subsequent licensed adaptation. Hence, while a programme idea usually lies at the heart of what is licensed, nevertheless, a format is both more and different to the programme idea. Rather, as has already been suggested, it is an interlocking package of programme-related knowledges which increase the adaptability of the programme that a company licenses to another producer.

Put another way, the business of a TV programme format distributor is distribution not production. What such a company circulates is the unique combination of information and experience organized around the adaptation and remaking of a particular television programme. In turn, it is the licensee rather than the licensor that is vitally concerned with the ratings success or otherwise of the adaptation when it is broadcast to the viewing public. This is not, of course, to suggest that the latter is uninterested in the fate of the adaptation. Clearly, the continued success of adaptations helps maintain and enhance the reputation of the format service. However, the format licensor's business arrangement is with licensees not with the viewing public. With this qualification in mind, one can continue tracing the process whereby the TV programme format comes into full existence and maturity.

Post-broadcast assembly

Once an initial production of the programme has successfully gone to air, then it becomes possible and necessary for the format owner to set about systematically assembling various knowledges that have attached to the emerging TV programme format. As the past two chapters have suggested, several documentations of these knowledges already exist and these are now methodically organized and elaborated. Among the items already given concrete form are the 'long-form' and the 'short-form' of the paper format as well as one or more video recordings either of broadcast programmes or of office or studio pilots. In turn, the successful first screening of the programme based on the format helps provide further documentation of the knowledges that will be knitted together to help form the full programme format.

What, then, are these knowledges? We can identify at least ten areas of the operation of production, finance, broadcast, marketing and distribution that by this stage are capable of being interrogated to yield documentation. They are:

1. Production and broadcast notes. During and after the programme's making and broadcast, steps are taken to ensure the writing up of the different stages, including outlining the resources deployed in this process. Such a record not only registers what took place in production and broadcast but it will also serve as a guide for future adaptations.

2. Revenue. Formats are as much to do with finance and income as they are to do with production. Hence another element that must be recorded on paper is complete detail on the income streams that were activated around the programme.

3. Broadcasting also furnishes off-air recordings of one or more episodes of the programme, yet another important repository of practical information and know-how.

4. Even if the programme was not scripted, nevertheless it is now possible to compile post-production scripts as further vehicles of industrial knowledge and service. On the other hand, if the programme was scripted, then such scripts become part of the full programme format package. And while 'live' programmes such as a reality show may not have scripts, nevertheless, they frequently have breakdowns of every episode such that a would-be licensee can understand what happens over, say, thirteen weeks.

5. Budget information. Obviously this concerns pre-production, production itself and post - production as well as other costs associated with providing some of the elements necessary for the programme. Hence, for example, with the New Zealand format for a makeover programme, *Dream House*, the format included

extensively written information on the costs of buying two houses that would become the objects of the makeover as well as costs of material and tradesmen together with finances to be recouped through the later sale of one of the houses.

6. Audience ratings and demographic information. This will constitute crucial knowledge for the future so far as episode length, timeslot, day of screening, specific audience appeal and so on are concerned. It is also one further means for a future format licensee to gain a fuller understanding of the specific nature of the format.

7. Sponsors and advertisers. Based on the initial broadcast arrangements, it should be possible to formulate how a particular advertiser might reach a clearly defined and precisely targeted audience with an adaptation programme. Additionally, this knowledge should also instruct in how to set an advertising budget including where to spend it and show the best returns on investment.

8. The original broadcast also generates various materials in the way of stills, text, sound and image to do with publicity, advertising and other marketing stories and information. Together, these help brand the programme. It may also be possible because of this first-run to identify further marketing opportunities. Collectively, this cluster constitutes an important level of business knowledge forming the format.

9. Merchandising and other cross platform opportunities. Under the name of interactivity, the latter is becoming an increasingly important revenue generator around such technologies as gaming, messaging, and telephony.

10. Additionally, knowledge and awareness about organizing and streamlining production and broadcasting. These results come together in a living form in key industry personnel, most especially the producer. In turn, she or he is now capable of becoming a consultant to a further adaptation of the format. A consultancy may be straightforward or it may be more complicated. For example, with a game show, especially the older, more classic ones such as *Wheel of Fortune* and *Jeopardy*, consultation will occur when the initial format adaptation is taking place. Once the programme is up and running, there is little involvement apart from some quality monitoring and occasional doctoring. However, with 'live' programme formats that involve ordinary, non-professional on-screen figures, consultancy may be more complicated and ongoing.

Finally, too, this first production and broadcast also yields other materials that can be deployed in subsequent adaptations. Hence, for example, there may be specialist software, computer graphics, digital special effects, recorded music and theme or programme songs and tunes. These can be assembled into the interlocking package that is the TV programme format. There may even be more material format resources such as special equipment or even sets, properties and costumes. As items available for hire, these also become part of the larger format licensing arrangement.

In any case, though, the devisor/owner is now in position to put together the major written document in the format's development. Following the earlier stages of the initial written format concept and the paper format, the opportunity is now at hand to assemble the format Bible. Attention now turns to this element.

The Format Bible

As already suggested, a format's first producer and/or owner will be heavily involved in helping to compile the written Bible. S/he will have the different technical people write up or guide the writing up of whatever stage or element that they were responsible for in the initial adaptation. In turn, these pages are collated into the master document - a kind of complete, blueprint or encyclopedia that should answer every question that a licensee adaptor might have about the programme format. In the past, this particular dossier was often referred to as the Production Guide or Format Guide. Nowadays, the manual is increasingly known as the Production or Format Bible. Where once, TV programme distributors used the notion of the sacred book of Christianity to refer only to scheduling, ratings and demographic information, the term Bible is now being used in a more inclusive way. The Format Bible refers not only to audiences but also covers other important areas of a format's manifestation to do with production, finance, marketing and distribution.

By way of example of what makes up one of these blueprints, I will look briefly at two format Bibles that cover two different kinds of 'live' programme. The first had to do with a chat show while the second involved a game show. More importantly, the first Bible is a relatively slim document in keeping with the fact that the adaptation based on the format had only had one broadcast airing in the home territory. By contrast, the second Bible is much bulkier, displaying a comparable enlargement of documentation. This was a sign both of the fact that the format had been adapted in many territories and that additional notation was therefore possible and necessary.

1. The *Room 101* Bible

This was the format for a light entertainment series broadcast on BBC2 in the UK in 1994. The programme was described as a chat based comedy show that each week featured a celebrity guest star. Subsequently, in 1995, the programme was 'formatted'. This activity not only involved the process of format documentation but also included obtaining the legal clearing of rights and subsidiary matters. By documenting the elements of production, broadcasting and marketing that had already taken place with the original UK programme, BBC WorldWide (Formats) turned this into a package of knowledge that could be distributed internationally.

The Format Guide was *Room 101*'s Bible. Altogether, it runs to 58 pages (although several of these consist of no more than a short paragraph and a large amount of blank space). In any case, most of the material is a set of post production scripts (31 pages). While not carrying any table of contents, the dossier includes general notes on the host, the guest, the 'rules' of the show, the set and the

Figure 5.1 Cover of the *Room 101* Bible

individuals that make up the production team (five pages). A second section deals with the organization of time in the production process and includes descriptions of how an episode is researched, how choices are finalized, scripting, timetabling the studio day (five pages). Matters to do with studio plan and the set runs to seven pages, mostly drawings, including a floor plan insert. Yet another part of the Guide deals with the budget and a profile of viewers based on audience research associated with the UK production (seven pages). Finally the package also contains a sample post-production script based on a UK episode.

Meanwhile, a note on the cover of the Guide indicates further elements of the overall package that are available to a format licensee. These consist of Consultancy ('Advice and guidance throughout the production process'); Design ('Studio plans and set design'); and, Video Cassette ('BBC programmes for reference and inspiration'). The front page of the dossier summarizes the benefits of the package

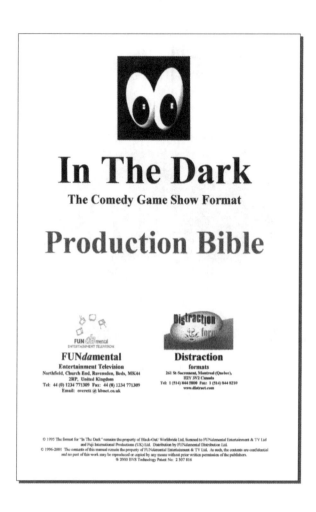

Figure 5.2 Cover of the *In the Dark* Bible

that is the format: 'Repeat the winning formula - create your own successful series of *Room 101* with BBC World Wide Television's format package'.

2. The *In The Dark* Bible

By contrast with *Room 101*, this programme is a game show. As it's Bible explains:

> In The Dark *is the hilarious game show format that allows the viewer at home, and in the studio audience, to see in the dark! This is possible due to the revolutionary and patented BVS (Beyond the Visible Spectrum) technology. The standard format features 3 couples competing in crazy challenges & games in absolute pitch darkness.*

With an earlier working title of *Black Out*, the format was devised by John Gough and Mark Overett. The original UK pilot on which the Bible is based was developed by Fundamental Entertainment Television and Fuji International Productions

Figure 5.3 The *In the Dark* Bible includes merchandising

(UK). The programme went to air on ITV in 1996 and later screened on Channel 5. By 2001, when the Production Bible or Manual that I was able to consult had been assembled, the format had been adapted in some 27 different national territories. These centered on western Europe, stretching from the United Kingdom across to Poland, Russia and the Ukraine and running from the Scandinavian countries in the north to Spain, Portugal, Italy and Turkey in the south. Meanwhile, across the Atlantic, *In The Dark* has appeared in Canada, the United States, Brazil and Argentina. It was also adapted in Australia and New Zealand. Altogether more than 350 episodes of the programme have been produced worldwide.

In other words, even by 2001, the format of *In The Dark* was more mature and developed as a blueprint than its *Room 101* counterpart. This was clear from the appearance and size of *In The Dark's* Production Bible. The manual consists of approximately 196 pages that include additional handwritten notes but does not include further notations and small addenda that had not yet been incorporated into the text. There is little blank white space in the text. Instead, the great majority of pages are full of printed information while others combine text with coloured illustrative pictures or graphics. Some 33 of these pages contained full-size or half-size colour photos that further exemplify and illustrate points mentioned in the text or else help document particular versions of the programme produced in different territories. In addition, there is also a double A3 size foldout scenic design incorporated into the manual.

The Contents page of the Bible indicates that these pages were divided into 37 sections that were collected together into six major parts. These have to do with an introductory overview (four sections), the see-in-the-dark technology (three), pre-production (five), production (ten), how the show is played (six), and additional matters including ratings, demographics, marketing and published feature articles (nine). Like *Room 101*'s Bible, this one also contained samples both of a Running Order and a RX Schedule. On top of this, because various different kinds of games can be played, a total of 72 specific games are set out in the 'How do you play the show?' section ('from obstacle courses and sports to messy-food-paint-games, make-up to fancy dress and sexy innuendo games').

The Bible devotes most space and attention to the actual making of the programme. The 'Your Show in Production' part consists of information about the following:

- Front of set
- The dark room
- Props
- Sound
- Host profile
- Host assistant profile
- Music
- Graphics
- Clothing and costumes
- Make-up

Because all this amounts to a piecrust framework for a changing series of games, the devisor/owners were the first to recognize that the format could not be rigidly applied everywhere but must be ready to change and adapt. As a note in the Introduction points out:

> *Obviously individual territories may need to amend the length of individual games or segments to suit the real timing of their 1/2 hour or 1 hour programme. As the* In The Dark *format is a flexible one, some producers may wish to look at making changes to suit their specific cultural or geographic location.*

Because of a format's success in a large number of territories, then - on top of what might be contained in this kind of dossier - it also becomes possible to provide a second kind of Bible, the video Bible. This was the case with *In The Dark* where Distraction, who had become the international distributor of the format, made available a video package, containing as many as twelve different programme elements and full programmes from different territories. Over and above these resources, two different kinds of consultancy services were also mentioned in the Bible. The first was the production consultancy service offered in the person of the two devisors. Meanwhile, the second service had to do with the necessary hire of the BVS technology and an operator.

Summing up, then, as a comparison of the Bibles for *Room 101* and *In The Dark* suggest, a format package is always, potentially at least, less than fully matured, incomplete, ever ready to incorporate further elements depending on experience in any particular territory and what the registered owners seek to document from that specific experience. In any case, a Bible will include many, although not all, of the elements in a TV programme format. It is itself only a part - although a major one - of the total package of knowledges that is the format. The point of the latter is only incidentally to help make a TV programme. Rather, it is put together in order to produce a product, a business service. I now move on to the circulation of this commodity.

Distributing the TV programme format

In addition to written material including studio floor plans, set designs, production drawings and so on, there may be other graphic and software materials, not to mention video promotions, show-reels, film footage and so on that form the total format package. As has been noticed above, components such as off-air recordings and consultancy services are other parts of the same parcel of knowledge that exist outside the written form of the Bible. The importance of these non-Bible based knowledges should not be underestimated. Chapter 3 noted that what was crucial in the package with the licensing in 2000 of the *Coronation Street* format to China for the making of *Joy Luck Street*, for example, was not a Bible but rather the extended engagement of the services of an executive producer from the United Kingdom. Long experienced with the British soap opera, this producer helped the Hong Kong-based Ya Huan Audio and Video Production Company and the Bejing Broadcasting Institute to set up the production system to make a daily television soap opera that very loosely resembled *Coronation Street*.

In any case, as well as recognizing the significance of all the elements in a format not just what seems to be a production recipe, it is also important to stress the fact that while the format elements are possibly unremarkable in themselves, what matters is the marketing mix of these, the process of bringing together and welding these in a unique way. In other words, the programme format - the total system of elements - is characterized by functionally interdependent parts. The TV programme format consists not only of particular knowledges but their unique organization.

With this organized system of knowledge in place, the owner now sets about distributing the format to would-be licensees in other territories to enable the production of authorized adaptations. Although the broadcaster - who provided the first programme production commission - may have a share in the ownership of the format, nevertheless, that group is, usually, happy to leave the task of international distribution either to the production company if the latter has such an arm or to enter into other arrangements preferably with companies with international linkages.

The reasons are obvious. After all, the devisor/developer has the intimate production experience that will probably come into play in any licensing and adaptation. In addition, the broadcaster only owns a share in the format rights. Finally, too, the format owner may have an on-going distribution agency, which can, more easily, handle this marketing.

In practice, a large number of format owners prefer to handle their own distribution. Consequently, there are only a handful of format distribution specialists. Chapter 7 reveals in more detail that Distraction is one of the few companies to completely limit its business to that of distributing TV programme formats. In point of fact, though, format distribution is not as easy or as economical as it may look. As one programme format devisor suggested, 'sometimes programme distributors have been tempted into this market but they have quickly discovered that it is different to that of programme marketing' (Overett 2002). In any case, format owners often shy away from the handful of distributing outlets in favour of setting up their own distribution company and handling their own formats. Hence, for instance, Julie Christy of Touchdown Productions has followed this course of action by setting up her own distribution outlet. And, of course, while some of the larger companies will also distribute the formats of others, these are less likely to receive the energy and attention that the company might bestow on the distribution of its own formats (Rodrigue 2002).

Upfront costs to the distributor in selling include duplication and that of maintaining a stand at such markets as that of MIPTV at Cannes. Hence, this kind of distributor may be inclined towards charging the format devisor some 50 per cent off the top including costs. In addition, distributing formats usually involves on-going relationships between the distributor and the licensee/adapter. Frequently the distributor will go along to the production wherever it may be in order to undertake a 'handholding' exercise.

As a further stage in the process being traced, the format now becomes the basis of a commercial relationship between two business organizations usually located in different parts of the world. Here, I postpone until the next chapter the matter of the markets where licensor and licensee can come into contact. One should also note in passing that several of the larger transnational format companies are vertically integrated business entities so that adaptations of their formats in a particular territory will be undertaken by a branch company or joint venture partner rather than a licensed independent producer.

It is also worth mentioning here the fact that piracy plays an important parallel role to licensing in the distribution of programme formats. Frequently, though, these unauthorized adaptations are the result of only limited access to the body of business knowledge that is the TV programme format. Instead, the unauthorized adapter has had to rely on only one or two components, usually off-air recordings of a previous adaptation. Using that or some other element as foundation, the unlicensed producer then attempts to recreate the programme format as the basis of an adaptation. While such adaptations often involve shrewd guesses at particular production knowledges, frequently this kind of adapter obtains little grasp on the various other knowledges that make up the format.

In any case, a truism in the business is that the more elaborate the knowledges contained in a format are then the harder it is to pirate and the easier it is to protect. Very often, the format knowledges gleaned from broadcast episodes: may fail to realize and include vital elements in the overall package to the detriment of the pirate producer.

Like other commercial marriages in the 'business format' franchising business, it is the legal contract that binds the business relationship of licensor and licensee. More is said about the legal basis of these contracts in Chapter 9. Nevertheless, it is useful to note some of the more important features of deals between licensor and licensee including fee structures.

Fees and deals

Up to this point, I have indicated several contractual arrangements entered into by the different parties concerning formats and it is useful now to provide further details. Among the matters designated in such deals are the various rights attaching to different elements, territories, production obligations and time periods.

Generally, a format licensing deal will only cover the free-to-air rights and will not include PayTV rights although the format owner might decide to include these to win something particular from the other party (Franken in Adair and Moran 2004). Ancillary rights such as those to do with merchandising, SMS and other phone voting revenues are also important and can often be a significant source of revenue (Gough 2002; Levine 2003). A typical deal concerning these might involve a fifty-fifty per cent split between the owner and the licensing broadcaster. Memos have even been known to assign a percentage of a winner's earnings to the licensor such as the situation where the devisor/owner of *American Idol* gets 20 per cent of the winner's earnings (Anon. 2002c).

When it comes to international format deals, the world is divided into a series of approximately five regional markets. First of these is a set of national territories principally among the larger populations of Western Europe such as Germany and France but also including Japan. A common licensing fee might amount to $20-30,000 per episode. Second is a more amorphous group that includes other parts of Western Europe and Australia with fees running at approximately half that of the first group. The next market includes territories in the former Soviet block and pays approximately $1,000 per episode. Next comes other smaller or less lucrative territories such as Uruguay, Turkey and even PR China which, at best, only return about a quarter of the previous region's revenues. Meanwhile, the last region is that of the United States where the returns for licensing fees are very high indeed and worth more than all these other territories combined. Hence, the general advice to devisors and developers in striking any distribution deal is to hang on to the latter rights at all costs, isolate the United States from whatever deal is done involving the rest of the world (Adair & Moran 2004).

Sometimes, in order to obtain the local broadcast rights to a programme, a broadcaster is often required to pay a licensing fee for a format adaptation and is forced to make a local version of the programme. Thus, this licensing broadcaster ends up paying twice, once for the broadcast of the overseas original and once for the licensed adaptation of a local version.

Additionally, there may also be a signing fee. Formats are sometimes secured by contract when the network has no intention of making the programme in question. Instead, the aim is to prevent the property falling into the hands of rival broadcasters. To obviate the fact that there may be no production and therefore no license fee for each episode, the devisor secures a fee in this alternate way.

Finally, it is also valuable to recognize that a memo deal concerning formats will always include a specified time period. A standard licensing deal would be for three years with another three-year option. If the broadcaster does not make the programme within this time frame, then the licensing rights revert to the developer. A renewal clause will specify that on the day after the last broadcast of the format, the broadcaster must sign a renewal for the licence with fees rising by a specified percentage. If the broadcaster does not sign, then the licensor will take the format to rivals.

Adapting a format

Meanwhile, in the field of TV programme format distribution, a key question is how much flexibility is there in the application of the format. Some format owners, such as the BBC with *The Weakest Link*, insist on complete adherence to the format so that all programme adaptations bear very close resemblance to the original and to each other. Similarly, Celador with *Who Wants to be A Millionaire?* insist that there be a strict adherence to the details laid down in the production Bible, even down to such matters as the colours of the set.

Even where the licensee is not under the same strict obligation, there is often a general reluctance to vary the knowledges and experience in the format. Indeed, there are many who hold to the motto 'the biggest do is a don't'. As David Lyle, formerly with Fremantlemedia put it, 'Don't improve the show backwards' (Buneau 2000). In other words, the licensing company should remember that it acquired a format probably because it was successful and appealing, so why then attempt to interfere with the elements that presumably brought this about?

As part of this continuity, many format owners assume and expect that their producers will have a direct and continuing consultative involvement with the production of the adaptation. Anna Bråkenhielm, managing director of Strix Television put it like this:

> We don't only sell licenses, we go out and co-produce. There's always a big exchange between our producers and the new producers. You should go out like a missionary and teach other people. I think it's more and more important to have a production experience. (Kingsley 2003)

In licensing a format, a producer is, frequently, allowed a deal of flexibility so far as the choice and arrangement of elements in the adaptation is concerned (Goodwin 2001). There is a recognition that the original set of knowledges and their organization may have to be varied to fit production resources, channel image, buyer preference and so on. Mark Overett offered an example of this kind of thing:

> At the moment our ideal commission is 26 shows for In The Dark. It's about thirteen shows per year, we can sustain that quite happily and the ratings will hold. Romania is signing for 120 shows. I am buggered if I know how we are going to handle that because In The Dark is basically a one hit show format. (Overett 2002)

Figure 5.4 An Italian adaptation of *Celebrity Survivor* ©Castaway Television

In other words, the original production of the format does not have to be slavishly imitated but rather serves as a general framework or guide within which it is possible to introduce various changes. Peter Langenberg from Endemol once described a format adaptation as a balancing act between the commitment of the format owner and the wishes of the licensee - 'Never, ever say "this is the way we did it so this is the way you must do it"' (Wit 2001).

This does not mean that the format is simply a loose guide that is open to major negotiation between owner and licensee. Owners have been known to refuse a request to vary even one element in a format. After all, as they might explain to the licensee, that component is what makes the programme work. The devisor and developer know this from their experience with the format so that the licensee needs to accept this on faith.

At the same time, the continued distribution and adaptation of formats over time often leads to significant variation and development. With *In The Dark*, for example, continued distribution and adaptation led to the situation already described where the format proceeded to gather more and more new elements including, in France, metamorphosing into another format called *Guess Who's Coming To Dinner*.

Significantly, under standard format licensing agreement, these variations and additions to a television format developed through adaptation become a further part of the format with ownership vested in the original licensor. Clearly, under this type of permitted variation, there is no veneration of or long-term respect shown to the early version of a format. Rather, as has already been noticed in the development phase, the format is seen as a loose and expanding set of possibilities across the fields of production, finance, marketing and broadcast. There is, on the part of the format owner, the overriding imperative to gain maximum commercial advantage from everything generated from the initial set of elements. In turn, the new elements introduced as variations in the adaptation will be equally as available as the original should a further adaptation of the programme format be required. Thus, by way of an additional example, a South American version of Fremantlemedia's *Man O Man*, prepared for broadcasters in Argentina, Uruguay and Paraguay in 1996/7, drew as much on an Italian version of the format, *Beato tra la donne*, as it did on the German original (Moran 1998: 122-4).

These remarks about format adaptation, then, conclude this sketch of the genesis and making of TV programme formats. Over the past three chapters, I have traced the steps whereby the format evolves from an initial impulse or idea into a collected body of industry knowledge that facilitate the making of the same programme often with significant variations in different territories across the world. This kind of trajectory implies linkages that stretch across large parts of the world from, say, the devisor and developer in The Netherlands to the producer and broadcaster in India. In other words, the format business occurs on a global scale and it is to other features of this kind of transnational network that I turn to in the next chapter.

CHAPTER 6

Agents and markets

It's impossible to do without agents. The US market is so complex; you'd get eaten alive if you negotiated your own deals.

David Frank, RDF Managing Director (Tyreel 2002: 15)

Again it's a case of networking. It's not good enough to go to the market once. You have to go to the market ten times before they say - 'Good to see you again - I've been thinking about what you said last market'. Because it's not going to happen straight away. It's going to take years for that person working at home to get something up.

Mark Overett, Format Devisor and Developer (Interview Moran 2002)

Once a TV programme format is in place and ready to be licensed in different international territories, the owner seeks to distribute it to other television territories across the world. One of the most practical ways of doing this is to take the format to the international markets and festivals to find potential licensees based in these other places who are also at the markets. However, before looking more closely at this kind of event, one might pause to briefly note another significant intermediary in the system that facilitates international distribution of the TV programme format.

The importance of agents in helping to facilitate relations between devisors, developers and broadcasters has already been noted. Agents operate in the middle ground and help develop and maintain partnerships between often quite different bodies. As has already been suggested, they are important in several parts of the TV format field including that of international marketing.

Agents

While agents occur across the whole spectrum of the entertainment industries, they are - in the field of TV programme formats - significant intermediaries between different elements in development and distribution. Often taking a commission of up to 10 per cent of the episode format fee once a programme is up and running, agents in this field act as go-betweens, operating between the format owner and those who would license their formats. Agents can open doors to the larger broadcasters that devisors and owners cannot budge otherwise. However, some format devisors and developers that were consulted felt that agents are only necessary when a deviser and his/her formats are in high demand. In fact, some devisors have found that even in the event that an agency does become a representative, the agency will be mostly active on behalf of those devisors with high profiles and strong business reputations. Put another way, most independent format devisors feel that they do not need an agent. In any case, in smaller markets such as that of Australia, there is no such thing as agents who represent format devisors.

Such figures only operate in the more lucrative markets, most especially that of the United States.

If agents have, for many years, represented devisors in these markets, they have, more recently, begun to represent particular TV programme formats. In 2002, for example the BBC announced that it had signed a deal with Reville, a subsidiary of Universal, to develop scripted comedy and drama, a move which was also anticipated as leading to format deals. The arrangement was brokered by Ben Silverman who headed the company (Sanghera 2002; BBC 2003).

Meanwhile, the format distribution company, Distraction, announced that the William Morris Agency (WMA) would represent several of its formats in the US market including *Guess Who's Coming To Dinner?, In The Dark* and *The Ugly Duckling*. In line with the roles of agents in other areas of the entertainment industries, this company would take a pro-active role in relation to the formats. Under this kind of deal, WMA would work to package the Distraction formats with production companies, talent and other necessary elements to secure placement on US television (Distraction 2003).

Ben Silverman himself was the original trail-blazer so far as this very active agency role in format distribution is concerned. Beginning in 1996 while he worked at the UK office of WMA, it was his idea to put together a complete programme, including formats that had already been developed and broadcast in western Europe, experienced American producers and sometimes even stars, and sell this as a single package to one of the US networks (Goldsmith 2001). Even today, there are only a handful of agencies that specialize in this kind of brokering of TV programme formats.

So who are the principal agencies? Numbered among their ranks are the Creative Artists' Agency (CAA) based in Los Angeles, International Creative Management and two relative newcomers, the United Talent Agency and the Endeavour Agency (Grantham 2003). Still, it is the New York and Los Angeles-based King World and WMA which are the biggest. The latter is, probably, the most active in the market and has branches internationally, including one in London. In addition, in the United States particularly, entertainment lawyers also double up as agents (Idato 2004).

As already noted, agents in the field of TV formats, like intermediaries in other fields, tend to be most active on behalf of their most successful clients, thus ensuring that their efforts generate the most profitable outcomes. Commission for an agent who has brokered a format deal is typically 5-10 per cent of the budget. The better and more respected agents, especially in a market such as that of the United States, will have good contacts and high credibility with the important companies, most especially the broadcast networks. In turn, in order to protect this reputation, the agent herself or himself will act as a kind of customer to the format owner. The latter will need to be pitched to and convinced of the value of a new format before s/he will set up a three-way meeting between agent, owner/producer and the broadcasters (Grantham 2003).

Yet deals can go wrong even when a company works with an experienced agent. UK Celador, for instance, signed a contract with US ABC concerning *Who Wants to be a Millionaire?* However, in retrospect, the company felt it lost important controls on its format. The deal, brokered by an agent, allowed the broadcaster to control the number of episodes being produced. Looking back, Celador came to realize that this had been a mistake and was, probably, the reason that the programme only ran two seasons on the network (Bart 2000; Anon. 2003).

When it comes to distributing TV programme formats to other territories across the world, there are usually no broker figures involved. Instead the business deal is a direct one between format licensor and licensee. The annual cycle of TV markets and festivals (see Figure 6.1) is the best and most efficient means for putting these bodies in direct touch with each other. However, before looking at these trade events in more detail, it is useful to remember that these occur for a variety of commercial reasons. The markets are opportunities for those in film and television as well as new media to make different kinds of deals including those to do with finance, production and distribution. TV programme format exchange is only one of the many things that occurs at the fairs but, nevertheless, very important for present purposes.

The markets have been relatively slow to develop and have only reached their present strength in very recent years. With the earlier exception of US commercial network television, broadcasters everywhere have, historically, relied on various amounts of imported programming in their schedule. Hence, since the early 1950s, TV operators have looked to the international trading of programmes. At first, much of this was done on an ad hoc, one-to-one basis, often proving to be cumbersome and inefficient. Beginning in the 1960s, various international television exhibitions, markets and festivals have developed whose basic function is to put those who wish to trade in both completed programmes and programme formats in touch with those who want to license these. Like all fairs, these festivals bring together the two components of any market, sellers and buyers. In particular, the festivals often

MONTH	TRADE EVENT	LOCATION
January	NAPTE	Las Vegas, USA
February	BBC Showcase	Brighton, UK
March	MIPDOC	Cannes, France
March/April	MIPTV	Cannes, France
May	Rose d'Or	Lucerne, Switzerland
May	Los Angeles TV Screenings	Los Angeles
June	DISCOP	Budapest, Hungary
July	Monte Carlo TV Festival	Monte Carlo
September/October	MIPCOM	Cannes, France
October	Junior MIPCOM	Cannes, France
December	MIPASIA/TV Asia	Singapore

Figure 6.1 – Annual Cycle of Trade Fairs and Festivals

extend preferential treatment to the sellers, given that they, in turn, attract the buyers.

There are important secondary reasons for those involved in the TV format business to attend the fairs. As a recent note on MIPCOM's website (MIPCOM 2003) puts it, the industry is there at the market in order to:

- Buy and sell TV programmes
- Develop long lasting business relationships for the months ahead
- Make new contacts
- Speed up negotiations
- Create partnerships
- Keep abreast of important changes affecting the audio sector

In other words, the markets and festivals are trade events where the industry comes together physically as opposed to being an industry with an electronic/Internet presence and jurisdiction. The necessity of being there is well summarized above by format devisor and developer Mark Overett. These exhibitions and festivals are generally not open to the public. Instead, the core attendees are from within television industries across the world and include broadcasters, production houses, regulatory authorities, public agencies that promote film and television, trade associations, firms involved in entertainment law, media representatives and journalists and government consuls, ambassadors and other public officials. For my purposes, the main players are producers, distributors and broadcasters, while subsidiary agents include government agencies, financiers, packagers, and sales agents.

Although drawn from all corners of the world, nevertheless there are a disproportionate number of participants from the United States, the United Kingdom and Western Europe. Over the years, there has been some variation in location, timing and scope of some of the exhibitions and markets although the major ones have been very durable. The most important ones are discussed below.

The showcase market

Before looking at those fairs and exhibitions where buyers and sellers come together in neutral space, controlled by a third party, it is worth starting with a different type of market organized around showcase screenings. The latter event is like a film or television festival that serves a country, a region or even a single company. Hence, in the present or in the past, there have been European independent, Nordic, German and French showcases, events designed to highlight new programming for would-be buyers. Nowadays, there are two really notable instances where sellers have the buyers come to them rather than both going to a neutral third space. These showcase markets happen in the United States and the United Kingdom respectively (Grantham 2003).

The Los Angeles May screenings

The first of these trade fairs occurs in Los Angeles in the months of either May or June. (Despite this minor variation in timing, the event continues to be known as the May screenings). This fair is a dispersed one. It operates by courtesy of the big television production companies headed by the major studios including Columbia, MGM and Disney, inviting the top international buyers to their premises in Los Angeles to see the next season's pilots.

Because the studios themselves are scattered around the Los Angeles area, a tradition has evolved whereby the companies coordinate their screening dates to avoid clashes. Meanwhile, the international buyers remain in central accommodation, many at the Century Plaza Hotel near the Twentieth Century Fox studios in Beverley Hills. Over consecutive days, for a week or more, the buyers are bussed from their hotels to the different studios for showcasings of the new season's programming. Here, they must guess which of the new Hollywood television programmes are capable of being successful with their own domestic audiences.

The BBC showcase
Some of these same buyers will have already visited the BBC's own trade fair, the BBC Showcase (BBC 2003). This four-day event is held annually in Brighton in February each year. The Showcase is the television programme sales market for BBC Worldwide. Begun in 1976, it is the world's largest programme market hosted by a single broadcaster. In 2003, for example, over 1,500 hours of programming including drama, entertainment, comedy, factual and documentary, children's and music was presented in the form of show-reels and full screenings. Format licensing is another key component of BBC business so that that same year the Romanian, Dutch, Chinese and Indian women hosts of *The Weakest Link* were on hand for a presentation. The Showcase also offers deals on new games and interactive services linked to digital platforms.

Gaining market advantage
With both the Los Angeles and Brighton fairs, there is on hand a large volume of new programmes and formats and a significant number of important buyers such that the seller can tailor the marketing pitch accordingly. Where buyers represent different networks and channels in the same territory, there is a danger that they might get into a bidding war that drives prices up. Major buyers frequently counter this. Agents or acquisition officers in Los Angeles or London will give them advanced advice about upcoming programming and formats such that they can strike early deals even before the screenings or Showcase. However, where these early events attract many hundreds of the larger buyers, it is the advent of the big markets a little later in the year that brings out both sellers and buyers in their thousands.

The trade markets

MIPTV
While some television markets are the initiative of trade associations or municipal or city authorities, these French markets are commercial exhibitions that regularly turn a handsome profit for their owner. Not surprisingly, theirs is the highest of

Figure 6.2 The Palais des Festivals in Cannes

tariffs for delegates. The most important of all the TV markets, MIPTV (Marché Internationale de Programme Télévisione - World Market for Television Programmes) was started in 1963 by French businessman Bernard Chevry. Although himself based in Cannes, the market made its first appearance in Lyons before switching to Cannes (Beauchamp & Behar 1992; Turan 2000; Grantham 2003).

The early 1960s was not an especially favourable time to begin a television market. Many national industries following public service models had only one or two channels in operation while television was only beginning in many smaller countries. In effect, television markets in many territories were quite restricted in their need for programming. However, Chevry's market soon caught on as did his music market begun in 1967. Indeed, the latter's name MIDEM, an acronym for the music market (Marché Internationale de Disc et Editione Musicale - World Market for Records and Music Publishing) became the parent company whose fairs included MIPTV.

In 1985, Chevry sold MIDEM Organizations to a UK company, Television Sound, who, four years later, sold it to Reed Publishing. Although the latter had begun as a paper manufacturer, it had expanded in several directions including media and trade exhibitions so that acquiring the two MIP fairs suited its purposes.

Based on the lunar calendar, MIPTV is held each year in March or April over six days in the Palais des Festivals in Cannes. In fact as is highlighted by the use of both French and English as the official languages of the market, two parallel events occur at MIPTV. The first is a meeting together of important elements of the Francophone television industries, most especially that of French television broadcasting. Leading executives from all the networks attend, as do many government officials, generally led by the Minister for Communications and Culture. In turn, news about French television and media made available publicly at MIPTV receives extensive coverage in the French media (Grantham 2003).

Meanwhile, the second parallel event is the one better known to the

Figure 6.3 The Endemol stand at MIPTV 2004

international television industry at large. This is the television exhibition which now attracts over 10,000 participants involved in TV broadcasting, programme production, distribution for TV, video and the Internet, advertising, licensing and merchandising, consultancy, service companies and new media. With over 2000 business firms being represented, there are now more than 500 stands in the main halls of the Palais. It is there as well as the hotel suites and private yachts that a great many business deals are struck. These are of four kinds: financing and co-production; distribution deals on finished programmes, films and so on; format licensing deals; and company take-overs.

Format deals have become increasingly important in the last decade and are now one of the main activities at MIPTV. However the exhibition is principally aimed at sellers and buyers who have a large volume of product. Words of warning about trying to license or sell single products on the MIPTV website are highly relevant to those who have come there hoping to distribute a single TV programme format:

> *For the documentary producer with a single documentary to sell, MIPTV can be a very frustrating and unproductive experience. The majority of potential buyers are actively working the market as sellers, the demand for one-off documentaries is limited, the lack of a product catalogue can make selling one film extremely difficult, and at a market as high-powered as this, the major buyers are looking to develop long-term relationships with regular suppliers.* (MIPTV 2003)

In the markets, according to one analyst, programming is frequently bought or rejected unseen based on company reputation or distributor clout (Cunningham 1996). Very broad, rough and ready. Generic expectations are in play. Buying decisions not central to the schedule are often made on such apparently arbitrary grounds. Conversely, there is a tradition among some European broadcasters of scrutinizing possible foreign acquisitions very closely. In such a situation, it is often extremely difficult for the new company, the offbeat project or the unusual format to find customers. Hence, the story is told of how, in 1993, the US documentary cable channel Discovery for its first foray as a seller brushed up its profile by dressing its stall as a movie set. Actors were employed to create live action scenarios around a World War Two theme to coincide with Discovery's use of Normandy landing documentaries as their flagship programmes (Cunningham 1997).

MIPCOM

Although more recent in inception than the spring exhibition, MIPCOM which was established in 1984 has rapidly become the latter's equal and is just as important to the international television industry. Held at the same venue, the Palais des Festivals in Cannes, in September and/or October each year, the market is slightly shorter than its counterpart, running for five days. Again, it was Bernard Chevry who began this market, one of several attempts to initiate new trade exhibitions under the umbrella of the MIFED Organizations. Chevry's hunch was that a fair could be created around the growing home video market. Hence, he decided to launch a fair akin to MIPTV where home video rights could be traded among the independents who briefly dominated the field.

In similar manner to MIPTV, so ran the thinking, the distributors/sellers would come to VIDCOM and set up their stands. Buyers would come and screen content. And then acquire the rights for their particular territories (Grantham 2003). In the event, however, the video buying market was only mildly interested in having its own trade convention.

Instead a number of elements came together to transform VIDCOM into MIPCOM. The US sellers had found the timing of MIPTV not to their liking. March and April predated their own May screenings and pilots were generally not ready for presentation until several months later. MIPTV only served them as a means of selling their back catalogue. However what really fuelled the speedy growth of this trade exhibition in the 1980s was the rapid expansion of channel capacity in television systems in many places, most especially in Europe. Cross-border satellite television and cable television linked with deregulation and the introduction of commercial broadcasting rapidly increased the need for more programming. Meanwhile, in the United States in the 1970s, the introduction of both the Financial Interest and Syndication Rules and the Prime Time Access Rules had brought about a significant increase in the volume of television programming available. The result was that the autumn fair grew rapidly so that it shortly assumed the same size and importance as MIPTV. VIDCOM was therefore recast as MIPCOM, allowing the latter to be marketed as an evolution from VIDCOM.

In practice, then, MIPCOM is much like MIPTV. Although usually one day shorter, there are substantially, the same number of individual participants and

Figure 6.4 Visitors at the MIPTV 2004

companies attending and the same number of deals are struck in the same areas as those already mentioned. Although the Hollywood studios are on hand earlier in the year, in September/October at MIPCOM, they have their new catalogues available so that business is especially brisk.

MILIA

One such MIFED Organizations new venture is that of MILIA (Marché International des Loisirs Interactifs et Nouveau Media - World Interactive Entertainment and New Media Market). Originally opening its doors in 1994, this forum actually began four years earlier as a global meeting point for content and technology licensing, cross platform distribution deals, and joint ventures with such adjacent markets as that of TV.

As part of demarcating the area of digital interactivity, the forum has systematically incorporated new events including New Talent Competition (1995); Broadband Day (1997); ITV showcase (1998); MILIA Games (1999); Think-Tank conferences (2000); Digital Buyers Programme (2002) and New Format (2003) (MILIA 2003).

Currently, the forum which now calls itself World Interactive Content for TV, Mobile, Broadband attracts over 1,400 content providers from the areas of digital entertainment, interactive TV, Internet and mobile and draws its participants from 722 companies in 48 countries. In 2004, MILIA piggybacked on MIPTV in the Palais des Festivals in Cannes running for two days later in the MIPTV week. Its World Interactive Content Forum consisted of conferences as well as various exhibits and events. The forum specializes in interactive digital content for Television, Broadband and Mobile telephony. Principal business is content and technology licensing, cross platform distribution deals, and joint ventures while introducing new synergies with the TV market.

Other MIP/Reed exhibitions

As organizations professionally involved in the business of trade exhibitions relating to the media, both MIFED and Reed have been eager to add further markets to their slate of annual industry events. Currently, besides MILIA, three other fairs are attached to MIPTV and MIPCOM as follows:

1. Junior MIPCOM - children's TV market

This mini market occurs over two days in October as a kind of sideshow to MIPCOM. As its name implies, the fair is dedicated to the buying and selling of children's television which falls into six particular genres - animation; drama/fiction; documentary; feature film; comedy; art/music/culture and game shows. Begun in 1991, Junior MIPCOM currently attracts approximately 200 buyers, 200 sellers and about 400 companies, making it big enough to continue but too small to become a stand-alone fair in its own right.

2. MIPDOC

If MIPTV provides the template for MIPCOM, then a mini market such as Junior MIPCOM forms the prototype for this exhibition. Running over two days in March or April, immediately before MIPTV itself, the exhibition concentrates on the buying and selling of documentary programmes in current affairs; history/ethnology; discoveries; science and knowledge; arts/music/culture; adventure; lifestyle; personal viewpoint; docusoap and educational. Originating in 1997, MIPDOC is slightly larger than Junior MIPCOM but intimately depends on the larger market for its success.

3. MIPASIA/Television Asia

Designed as an Asian version of MIPTV, this event was launched in 2000. However, a good deal of business doubt enveloped it, thanks in part to the fall in the value of Asian currencies, such that by its third meeting in Singapore in December 2002, the event bore the name Television Asia, subtitled the Asian Television Forum (Burnett 2002). Like the MIP fairs in Cannes, this event stressed its trade orientation of bringing together sellers and buyers, finance and producers, and linking up Asian broadcasters and producers with international TV distributors. Additionally, the event also equipped itself with a conference and workshop that addressed digital media and technology trends as well as an honorific side that included the Asian Television Awards and the Asian Animation exhibition.

4. NATPE

Easily the largest market and fair in the world with participants sometimes numbering as many as 30,000, the National Association of Television Programming Executives (NATPE) is a non-profit US trade association or grouping. NATPE maintains its own permanent secretariat and hosts an annual convention that is also a marketplace. In the past, the exhibition has been staged in different cities in the

United States including New Orleans and Los Angeles although beginning in 2004, it is permanently mounted in Las Vegas (NATPE 2004). Occurring in January, NATPE runs for four days as both a convention for its members and as a trade market. The latter includes as many as 300 stands of major companies and others in the main exhibition halls. Originating in 1963, the annual get-together began as a means for TV executives to interact and as a forum for the facilitation and interchange of ideas. As part of this legacy, NATPE remains dedicated to a market that is less expensive so far as attendance is concerned compared with MIPTV and MIPCOM. Previously, the event was a means of distributing television programming although it now focuses on all forms of content and serves all kinds of platforms. As its website proclaims: 'If you buy, sell, develop, finance, advertise, market or license content; implement technology; exploit rights; or leverage media assets, NATPE ... is the best place to be for success today and growth tomorrow' (NATPE 2004).

Recent years have seen a downturn in the size and scope of NATPE that has, in part, prompted the permanent location of the annual exhibition in Las Vegas. The downturn undoubtedly reflects various industry tendencies including company takeovers and mergers, a slump in advertising sales and a peeling off of some market business from the exhibition floor to that of the private hotel suite (Grantham 2003). Gone is much of the fanfare that once took place on the market floor such as the appearance of TV stars and other costumed promotional activity. Nonetheless, as against this hiccup, the fact is that Hollywood remains the centre of the international television and multimedia industries so that NATPE will continue to be a vital market event.

5. DISCOP

'Showcase' markets might be seen as one kind of peeling off of sellers and buyers from the central exhibitions such as those of MIP and NATPE. Another is the specialized market/festivals looked at in the next section. In between, there is yet another kind of specialized market such as that represented by DISCOP (Discount Programming). Begun in 1992, the market occurs annually in Budapest each year over three days in late June. Its mission is to cater for the needs of emergent markets, most especially those in Central and Eastern Europe, Central and South East Asia, India and China (DISCOP 2004). More specifically, the exhibition addresses itself to trade in TV programming and feature films, thematic channels, TV formats, telenovelas and interactive solutions. To cater to this range, DISCOP splits its activities into four different sections - programme showcase; new technology exhibition; TV formats market; and, an industry conference.

Under the DISCOP banner, it is also worth mentioning the first TV programme format market that the group held in Lisbon in February 2001. The intention was to establish a festival entirely devoted to this newest area of international trade in television. Unfortunately, the festival was not well attended and has not survived.

The market festivals

Over and above the trade exhibitions where the only real game in town is buying and selling, some events are organized around two different kinds of meeting - markets, the trade fairs and festivals of workshops and screenings of programmes and films either in competition or alone. The thinking behind this doubling is obvious - two attractions should draw more participants than one might. In practice, those on hand at stalls in the exhibition find that they are not free to attend festival events, workshops and screenings. Not surprisingly then, market/festivals are actually few in number and are not important in the diary of the international television industry. Nevertheless, as part of this overview, one can note the two most significant of these. They are the Rose d'Or and the Monte Carlo Television Festival.

Rose d'Or Festival

This event, begun in 1961, has been very much a public broadcaster's club. The founding idea of the festival was to create a forum wherein public service broadcasters from the United Kingdom and Europe could fill the gaps in their summer schedule by swapping Light Entertainment programming. Under the definition used by the festival organizers, Light Entertainment covers everything from circuses to comedy specials, from game shows to cartoons. Currently, Festival competitions are organized around seven categories - comedy; sitcom; reality; variety; music; game show; arts; and specials. The Festival has been held each year in May over six days in the Swiss town of Montreux on Lake Geneva. Recently, as part of a general move to expand the size and appeal of the Festival from being simply an industry event, the organizers have announced a relocation from Montreux to the nearby city of Lucerne. Meanwhile, as its name implies, the Rose d'Or functions as a competitive television festival of screenings and jury selections whose ultimate prize is the golden rose.

At the same time, there have also been regular attempts to expand the market side of the event. Chief among these have been the videoKiosks, booths that enable participants to sample and view programming from different parts of the world. All the same, the Rose d'Or Festival remains a minor event in the calendar of international television, attracting only a tenth of those who attend Cannes with only token involvement from the United States and Asia.

Monte Carlo Television Festival

Although initiated as the Monte Carlo Television Market and Festival in 1961, the same year that Rose d'Or began and two years ahead of MIPTV, this annual meeting has recently vacated the area of the trade exhibition in favour of a television festival of screenings and industry-related events. Designed to lure business and other visitors to the principality of Monaco, the Market and Festival event was originally scheduled in February. Ultimately it was this timing, a month or so in advance of MIPCOM, coupled with the fact that the organizers refused to expand the limited space available for the trade exhibition that led to industry neglect and the consequent decision to wind it up.

Since 2002, a revamped Monte Carlo Television Festival has been timed for the first weeks of July as a means of snagging early holidaymakers from the industry. The Festival, which runs over six days features publicity-grabbing international awards, premiere screenings, panels and workshops. In addition, it also features a small amount of market-related activity such as a one-day workshop on TV formats in 2002.

Overall, then, the annual round of TV markets helps define the television year so far as broadcasters and producers, including those active in the field of TV formats, are concerned. Going to the markets is one of several ways in which the world TV format business continues to maintain its global reach. As the MIP website already mentioned suggests, attending the markets brings licensors and licensees into regular contact, builds and helps maintain business relationships, enables broadcasters and producers to spot new trends and developments, and draws nationally-based industry figures into more international networks. In short, the markets function as a kind of club, and club membership is maintained and exercised through repeated attendance there.

Who, though, are the principal attendees at these fairs so far as the format trade is concerned? This book has already touched on some of the relationships and connections across the field. These are taken up again in the next chapter that looks at some of the more important companies who are frequently represented by agents and invariably present at the main fairs and markets.

CHAPTER 7

Companies

We aren't really a television producer at all anymore. We are a content provider for multiple platforms.

John De Mol, former head of Endemol (Endemol 2004)

Chapter 3 began with the lone figure of the format devisor as a point of instigation of formats. However, as I have also stressed, formats need the involvement of many hands in growing to maturity so that companies, both large and small, are an inevitable part of the landscape. Reference has been made in passing to a number of these companies operating in the field of TV programme formats. These vary in their operation so that it is useful to begin this company survey by outlining the different kinds of possible operations in which the various groups are involved (Rodrigue 2002). There are at least four distinct types as follows:

1. The vertically integrated transnational group exemplified by both Endemol and Fremantle. These have a large catalogue of formats that they own. Thanks to both outright ownership and also to joint venture arrangements, they have production offices in a string of territories across the world. In turn, such companies produce adaptations of their formats for local broadcasters in these territories.

2. King World and Columbia TriStar represent another kind of operation. Based in Los Angeles, they are mostly in the business of programme distribution. This kind of company does not have a large number of overseas offices although there are some. However, these are sales offices only. Format licensing is only a small part of their distribution business. Typically, this kind of company will license its formats to a particular network then hire a local producer while acting as production consultant. What emerges is a co-production format adaptation.

3. Yet another type of operation is the production company working in a specific territory which creates or buys formats. In turn, it produces adaptations of these. One example of this kind of company is the Swedish Strix discussed below. These and others are like the first type although they operate at a local, national level rather than at an international one.

4. Another category concerns companies that do not conform to any of these types. Two can be mentioned. The first is a company specializing in format distribution. Distraction is a notable example of this type. Meanwhile, the BBC constitutes a unique second subtype. The latter both creates formats in-house and co-develops and co-produces. In turn, the Corporation has a format distribution arm that markets these internationally.

Over and above these specific styles of company operations, it is also worth mentioning at the outset that several organizations have led a drive to form joint venture agreements in individual national markets. Such an arrangement not only helps the parent organization grow in size but it also enables it to derive revenue not only for its intellectual property in formats but also profit from production itself. One other motive is also frequently at work - to prevent the plagiarism of that company's formats in the territory in question.

Another point that is also worth making is the fact that while the companies discussed below are ostensibly in competition with each other, there will necessarily be national markets where they will enter into particular business arrangements. Companies, then, compete but also cooperate. Hence, for example, in the UK Celador and Fremantlemedia are in competition with each other and Celador which owns the format produces a UK version of *Who Wants to be a Millionaire?* for the ITV Channel 3 network. In Australia, on the other hand, Grundy Television, a subsidiary of Fremantle, produces the series for the Nine Network under a licensing arrangement with Celador.

As Bob Campbell, CEO of Screentime, explained: '...you do the best deals in the territories where people are expert in their field and where they can place it with broadcasters or, in many instances, deal with the broadcasters direct - so its horses for courses' (Interview Moran 2003).

Finally, before looking at particular companies in some detail, it is also worth noting the number, size and scope of those active in the international format business. In point of fact, the number of companies operating in different territories varies considerably. Altogether, for example, the 2004 MIPTV website listed details of 471 companies that had identified themselves as operating in the TV programme format and the interactive format business (see Appendix iv). Of these, there were 291 in Europe, including the United Kingdom while there were 68 in the United States and Canada, 12 in South America, 63 in Asia, 14 in the Middle East, 4 in Africa and 19 in Australia and New Zealand. In other words, even allowing for the fact that this particular television market was in the South of France and therefore more easily reached by European companies than by others, the topography of companies active in this field is very skewed towards Europe and the United Kingdom. In any case, the landscape is a varied and somewhat confusing one. Therefore, a short guide to the main companies is in order. These follow in alphabetic order.

Action Time

Action Time began life in 1978 as a UK based broker of US game shows for the different British broadcasting groups, most especially Granada (Moran 1998). Among its early US clients were Paramount and Ralph Edwards Productions. However, the US companies always had a preference for being represented abroad by US brokers so that, over time, the supply of these game shows dwindled. In 1987, Action Time was sold to Zenith, a division of Carlton Communications, and Paramount. Four years later, to facilitate Carlton's bid for an ITV franchise, Zenith put the company up for sale and a management buy-out occurred (Carlton 2003).

The management group ended up with 70 per cent of the shares and Carlton and Paramount took 15 per cent each.

In keeping with its early role as a broker of game show formats, Action Time initially had little in the way of production facilities for the UK market. However, the introduction of independent programme production that began in 1980 with the arrival of Channel 4, led Action Time to become a producer. In recent years, the company is responsible for making all its own programmes which it supplies to both the commercial and the public service broadcasters for transmission on terrestrial and satellite and cable systems (Frean 1995; Kingsley 2003).

But Action Time also had a strong format development side led by Stephen Leahy and Trish Kinane. With Carlton already having an earlier stake in Action Time, that group finally took it over completely in 2003 and Leahy and Kinnane left to form Ludus Productions. In the new arrangements, the company finds itself alongside Planet 24 and Carlton's online programme support arm as a content provider to the main group. It continues to concentrate on game show formats. In its 2003 catalogue, Action Time lists some 57 titles including *The Mole* and *Catchphrases*. It produced the former in the United Kingdom and distributes *Survivor* outside the United States.

BBC

The British Broadcasting Corporation (BBC) is, of course, a television broadcaster and producer. Its primary area of responsibility as a national public service broadcasting organization is to provide radio, television and other communication services in the United Kingdom. As a television broadcaster, the BBC produces approximately 50 per cent of its programmes in-house and buys the other 50 per cent of its British content from UK based packagers. Through both its own productions and through its buyings, the Corporation as a broadcaster finds itself producing and distributing formats developed by smaller production companies. Hence, for example, the format *Room 101*, already referred to in Chapters 4 and 6, was co-owned by the BBC and Hat Trick Productions (UK).

The BBC's marketing operation is designed to gain further revenues from the sale of programmes and other services internationally. Over the years, the Corporation has seen many of its programme ideas imitated by broadcasters, especially public service channels, in different parts of the world. As formatting, including licensing, developed, the Corporation began to set fees for the use of its programme ideas. The BBC's Format Licensing division was established in 1993 as a unit of BBC Worldwide Television, the marketing arm of the corporation with sales offices in New York, London, Paris, Cologne, Sydney and Hong Kong (Moran 1998).

For the Corporation, format licensing is less valuable than the licensing of finished programmes. In 1993, for example, the BBC had approximately 1,750 titles in its programme sales catalogue but only 83 titles in its format catalogue. However, the business of both is expanding rapidly. In 2003/4 BBC Worldwide achieved sales of £657m, thereby returning £141m to the Corporation, an increase of 14 per cent (BBC 2004). However, even as recently as 1997, the Format division was not in position to be involved in the production of its formats in other places. Instead, all

Figure 7.1 Cover of the BBC catalogue

it could offer overseas producers was the opportunity to observe the BBC's production of its own formats.

Clearly, the Corporation was losing out in the rapidly expanding trade. Hence, in 1999, BBC Worldwide developed a strategy with BBC Entertainment to invest more than £300,000 a year into the production of game show pilots. This strategy has resulted in successes in the United Kingdom and internationally with shows like *The Weakest Link*, *Friends Like These* and *Dog Eat Dog*. Because it deals directly with broadcasters, thereby gaining both a production and a licensing fee, the BBC is now heavily involved in production consultancy so far as the international adaptation of its formats is concerned. Among the formats being produced in other territories in recent years with assistance from BBC production teams are *The Weakest Link*, *Top of the Pops* and *Yes Minister* (BBC Worldwide 2003).

Celador International

Celador began life as a production company in the UK around 1993. It is best known for its smash hit game show *Who Wants to be a Millionaire?* As outlined in

Chapter 4, this was principally the brainchild of David Briggs, then working as an on-air host at a UK radio station. While running a 'Double your money' quiz segment on air, the idea began to grow for what would turn out to be *Millionaire*. Devising the format with Mike Whitehall and Steve Knight, Briggs worked on and refined the format idea for nearly two years. The format came to Celador who were involved in further development before taking it to ITV. The format's first adaptation began on air in 1998 and was immediately picked up by the ABC Network in the United States. Since then, *Who Wants to be a Millionaire?* has been adapted in over 80 different territories across the world making it the most successful TV game show format to emerge in recent years (Celador 2004). However, after its prime time success in the United States, it was dropped in 2002 by ABC and has begun to wane elsewhere. In the meantime, Celador International has continued to develop new formats, specializing in the area of game shows. Among their recent developments are *Brainiest*, *Gibberish*, *Popcorn*, *The People Versus* and *Chain of Thought* (Celador 2004).

Columbia TriStar

Like its counterpart in King World, this is a small operation within a much larger, well- known film and television distributor. Originally founded in Hollywood in 1924, Columbia Pictures quickly evolved into a proficient and profitable producer and distributor of B movies. As television networking developed in the 1940s, it enthusiastically embraced the new medium, setting up its own production company in 1948. With plenty of TV series to distribute, the company steered its way through the financially turbulent years between around 1950 and 1970. Concentrating on distribution for television and, later, of feature films, it found itself a central player in the new Hollywood of the 1970s and onwards. Today, Columbia TriStar is a Hollywood major with the international distribution of film and television programmes as a major component of its business operation. In that capacity it also has a small presence in the format distribution business thanks to a number of classic US game shows such as *The Price is Right*, *Family Feud*, *The Dating Game* and *The Newlywed Game*. Columbia TriStar handles the format licensing of these and others for territories outside the United States. Based in Los Angeles, this small operation keeps busy offering format licensing and consultancy services on these as well as a handful of older US sitcom formats (Anon. 1994b; Anon. 2002c).

Distraction

Emphasizing the extent to which the TV programme format business has to do with international distribution and adaptation rather than initial programme production, Distraction Formats is a company that specializes in the circulation of formats generally devised and owned by smaller groups in the international arena (Rodrigue 2002). Larger format companies have the capacity to achieve international distribution and adaptation of their formats, often using their own affiliates. Smaller companies enjoy no such advantage. Hence, the importance of a company such as Distraction.

The company's founder, Michel Rodrigue, began in television production in 1980 (2002). After working for a small TV station in Quebec, he started his own

Figure 7.2 Celador advertises on the MIPTV Catalogue

production company, specializing in variety and light entertainment. Attending MIP regularly, he became part of an informal network with other companies including Harry de Winter, IDTV, Joop van den Ende and Gestmusic. Spearheaded by Stephen Leahy from Action Time, the group was interested in the exchange of TV programme formats. In 1988, Leady formed Action Group to facilitate this kind of exchange. At its height, there were fourteen different producers in the group that met four times a year. These were opportunities to exchange information and to trade formats. The group eventually dissolved as the format business grew.

At this point, Rodrigue went out on his own. In 1996, he began to concentrate on format distribution. Distraction was launched the following year. The company's headquarters is in Montreal and it has branches in Paris and London with a representative in Hungary. In a format licensing deal, the company makes available not only vital production knowledge but also a great deal of expertise concerning a format and its production. Currently, Distraction has business in nearly 40 countries although the great bulk of this is in Europe. In the area of comedy, *Love Bites* has been one of its most successful comedies while, in game shows, *In The Dark*, has also been highly successful (Distraction 2003).

Endemol

Easily the largest group operating in the field of TV programme formats this company has witnessed astonishing growth over the past decade (2002; 2004). Its name is an amalgam of the names of two Dutch TV producers.

Around 1975, Joop van den Ende - a former stage actor - began his own company in the Netherlands, organizing theatrical productions and events (Moran 1998). By 1979, he had also begun to produce TV drama series for the Dutch public broadcasters. By the mid-1980s, Joop van den Ende's principal business lay in TV production. With the creation of the first commercial Dutch broadcaster in the shape of TV station Veronica in 1989, the company signed a three-year deal for a high volume slate of programmes for the broadcaster. Meanwhile, the opening up of new commercial TV networks in neighbouring TV industries, in western Europe led van den Ende and his company to realize that they could sell such formats as *The Soundmix Show*, *Mini Playback Show* and *Honeymoon Quiz* in Germany and the United Kingdom. By 1991, an affiliate was opened in Germany following a volume deal with RTL Television (Fuller 1994b).

At the same time, a rival and future partner had emerged in the home market. In 1979, John de Mol, formerly a TV director, set up his own production company (Moran 1998). Initially, the company made one-off specials for the Dutch TV broadcasters although, by 1984, it was also making weekly series. Large volume deals with Sky Channel and Dutch RTL4 followed and, by 1992, the company had also secured valuable contracts in Germany.

To facilitate further international expansion, Joop van den Ende and John de Mol announced a partnership deal in 1993 and a new company, Endemol, came into existence in early 1994 (Briel 2001). Under the plan, the existing Dutch companies remained in place in The Netherlands while Endemol became the international parent. Within two years, the company had offices in neighbouring Germany, Portugal, Spain and Belgium. It soon realized that instead of starting these from scratch, it was easier to acquire outlets in different territories through the takeover of existing companies.

To finance this expansion, Endemol was floated as a public company on the Dutch stock exchange in 1996. There followed further acquisitions such that by 2000, the group had companies in France, Italy and the United Kingdom. By this time, Endemol had discovered its jewel in the crown in the shape of *Big Brother*. The latter first went to air in The Netherlands in late 1999. Its overwhelming success there triggered adaptations elsewhere including the United States where Endemol signed an agreement with CBS.

Meanwhile, the group itself was changing. In 2000 van den Ende retired on the

Figure 7.3 Cover of Endemol's DVD catalogue

grounds of ill health. Almost immediately, Endemol was taken over by Spanish telecommunications giant Telefònica for €12b.

The intention was to provide content for broadcasting companies as well as for the Internet, third-generation mobile telephone and other distribution platforms. As the brains behind *Big Brother*, de Mol agreed to remain for a further five years. The theatrical business was sold off to van den Ende while the distribution arm was also sold. Instead, the plan was to concentrate on the production of content for TV and interactive networks.

Aware that the true value of such formats as *Big Brother* lay not in the license fees that they might return but in their production and the ancillary revenue streams that they generated, Endemol continued to build its worldwide string of production outlets. Joint venture agreements were the principal means of enabling it to link up with the strongest potential production partners in any particular territory (Endemol 2002; Endemol 2004). The case of collaborations in Brazil and Argentina is summarized below. Meanwhile, Endemol set up a series of other companies such as Endemol Mexico, Endemol USA, Endemol UK and Endemol Netherlands.

These acquisitions not only provide the group with new production arms but have also bought in a substantial number of other formats. The acquisition of the company B&B, for example, added Switzerland to several other European territories where an Endemol-affiliate holds the format production rights to *Who Wants to be a Millionaire?*

As noted, some of the group names in different territories were new, reflecting another aspect of company philosophy.

In late 2001, Endemol decided to begin a more conscious branding process involving all aspects of its operation. A new company logo was created. Additionally, the parent name came to the fore in many different territories.

Recent trading figures are hard to come by. However, we can note that over the first quarter of 2003, the Endemol group had a combined turnover of €616.4m. This was 7.2 per cent more than the same period of 2002. In the same year, more than 15,000 hours of television were produced, spread over approximately 400 different programme series. The Endemol library contains over 500 programme formats and the company employs about 3,300 fulltime employees (Endemol 2002).

Meantime, the company is looking to further expand its business as a content provider, including but also moving beyond television to other platforms such as the Internet and mobile activity. Messaging, for instance, delivers roughly one fifth of all revenue but this is expected to double. Indeed, some of Endemol's new offerings move beyond TV. In 2003/4, a personalized diet service began in Holland and Germany. Here, Endemol communicated daily with subscribers through SMS. This venture was based on the relative success of a previous service, in conjunction with an Endemol Dutch reality TV show, *Big Diet*, that had persuaded half the trial members to pay a set fee for two months of tips and advice. The new venture eliminated the TV broadcaster altogether (Endemol 2004).

Finally, too, mention should also be made of a further change at the top. In very late 2003, Joaquìn Afut Bonsfills was appointed head of Endemol. This was, in part, an anticipation of the fact that de Mol himself would be released from contractual obligations at the beginning of 2005 and could cease to have an active engagement with the company. However, even if the second of the two principals were to leave, there is no doubt about the company's ability to continue to grow.

Endemol Globo and Endemol Argentina

Previously the largest television producer of drama in Latin America, the Brazilian Globo is a national media organization which in the past achieved significant revenue from the international sales of its drama serials, especially its telenovelas (Moran 1998). Besides headquarters in Rio de Janiero, the company also had programme sales offices in London and Paris. In the 1980s and the 1990s, Globo achieved significant sales of telenovelas in Europe where they enjoyed popular success. In 1993, on the heels of this trade, Globo began marketing formats. Their first programme format offered for licensing was that of an interactive game show *Voce Decide* (You Decide), originally devised for the Brazilian market. Like Action Time's *Cluedo*, *Voce Decide* was a hybrid, an amalgamation of a game show with a fictional situation and story. By 1996, the format had given rise to 37 adaptations in different parts of the world although in every case Globo only received a license fee for its format (Moran 1998).

Clearly, Globo needed a steady supply of formats. To that end, it was prepared to enter into a joint venture agreement with the Dutch giant, Endemol. Thus, in February 2001, there occurred the creation of a new company, Endemol Globo (Globo 2001). Under the deal, the two shared 50 per cent each in profits deriving from the new company's activities in both the Portugese and Spanish language markets. In effect, the deal gave Endemol access to the largest market in Latin America in an arrangement with a highly experienced local producer. Globo, in turn, got access to Endemol's catalogue of over 400 formats, including *Big Brother*. In fact, the association represented the second incursion by Endemol in the Latin American market. Shortly before the deal with Globo, the Dutch company had acquired a majority stake in the company P&P, an Argentinean producer. The new company is known as Endemol Argentina (Endemol 2002).

Fremantlemedia

Like Endemol, this company has followed a path of deliberate and aggressive expansion in the global TV production marketplace in the past decade. This course of action has worked so that, today, Fremantlemedia is second only to Endemol in importance in the international TV format trade (Fremantle 2003).

The company's expansion strategy has been based on its very large catalogue of drama and game show formats that it began to acquire from the early 1990s onwards (Moran 1998). Fremantlemedia was previously known as Pearson Television and was itself a subsidiary of the UK media and publishing group Pearson Plc.

In 1993, the parent bought Thames Television, formerly a broadcaster/producer and more recently the maker of such programmes as *The Bill*, *This Is Your Life* and *Wish You Were Here*.

Pearson Television was established in 1995 following the acquisition of Grundy World Wide. The latter had originated in Australia and had become a transnational production company with a particular specialism in game shows and daily soaps. Its operations were conducted across all five continents. Additionally, in 1997, Pearson acquired All American Television which itself had recently picked up the Mark Goodson catalogue of classic US game shows. These included *The Price Is Right* and *Family Feud*.

In mid 2000, Pearson Television was itself taken over by the German CLT-UFA, the latter becoming the RTL group. Clearly, it could no longer use the Pearson name so that a new title was in order. Fremantle had been the name of a US distribution company acquired by AAT and the latter helped form the name of the new company. Meanwhile, with interests in 23 television channels and 14 radio stations in 9 European countries, RTL Group is the largest media group in Europe. The company is owned by the Bertelsmann AG, an integrated media and entertainment company originating in Germany (Fremantlemedia 2003).

Fremantlemedia has several notable strengths in the format business that make it second only to Endemol in wealth and power. Some of these relate to its

Figure 7.4 The Fremantle stand at MIPTV 2004

background. Through AAT, the company acquired the classic Goodson games shows and continues to produce different local versions of such formats as *The Price Is Right*, *Card Sharks* and *Family Feud*. Meanwhile from the Grundy takeover, it has such classic drama formats as those derived from *The Restless Years*, *Sons and Daughters* and *Prisoner: Cell Block H*. Adaptations of these have been or are in production in such territories as Germany, The Netherlands, Greece, Sweden, Finland and Indonesia. In addition, the company also licenses various sitcom formats including *The Honeymooners*, *I Love Lucy*, *Man About The House* and *Mother and Son* and has been especially successful with these in the former Communist countries in Eastern Europe (Cousins 2002).

Even more importantly, Fremantle Media retains a significant presence in the area of reality formats, most especially with their *Pop Idol* property. The latter has been enormously popular and successful on both sides of the Atlantic and in a string of other territories. Altogether, it seems to have the same kind of longevity as other classic reality formats such as *Survivor* and *Big Brother*. Put another way, the company looks like retaining an important presence in the format field in the foreseeable future.

Figure 7.5 Granada Television's logo

Granada

Granada's involvement in media dates back to the early days of UK broadcasting (Granada 2003). The company was incorporated in 1934 to acquire the theatre and cinema operations of Sidney Bernstein and his brother, Cecil. A year later, it was floated as a public company. In 1954, it was awarded one of the UK's first commercial television broadcasting licenses, for the North of England weekday franchise. In the 1960s, Granada (as it was now known) branched into adjacent businesses including TV rental, motorway service stations, and bingo. Since the early 1990s, the group has changed its orientation, selling off some of its business interests. However, it did acquire London Weekend Television, Yorkshire Tyne Tees Television, the ITV regional franchises of Anglia TV and Meridian Broadcasting, the production output of HTV Productions and Border Television (Hansen 2002).

With such a large set of programme producers to serve, Granada International is the largest distributing company in Europe and handles activities such as co-production, acquisition, and international video and DVD sales, as well as format licensing. As already mentioned in Chapter 3, the Hot House (previously known as the Greenhouse) is the format development unit at Granada. Among some of their more notable successes developed with LWT have been *Boot Camp* and *I'm A Survivor...Get Me Out of Here!* Other recent Granada formats have included *Cold Feet, Monster Garage, Look Of Lurve, Demolition Day* and *18-30 Stoners* (Granada 2003).

Finally, one should also mention the company's strategy regarding format distribution. As noted above, first option deals are important for companies that will have no other presence in a particular territory. Hence, in the absence of either operating a national branch or a joint venture agreement, this kind of arrangement is seen to work in favour of a format owner such as Granada. Here, the overseas company will be active in attempting to secure a production agreement with a local broadcaster whereupon the local company gets to produce the adaptation. Currently, Granada has this kind of arrangement in place with French Glem TV, Spanish Videomedia, Italy's Mediaset, Scandanavia's Nordisk Film and TeVe Holland.

IDTV

The import and export of programme formats has been, and still is, a particularly common, long-term market strategy among Dutch television producers. In addition to Endemol, there are a series of other smaller companies including Eyeworks TV and Harry de Winter Media. However, the second company from the Netherlands to be discussed here is mid range in size and, in the past at least, maintained a more 'quality' orientation in the marketplace, in line with both its own liberal left philosophy and the programming alignment of its principal clients, the Dutch public broadcasters.

IDTV was founded in 1979 by a former Dutch disc jockey who was also briefly involved through his company, Inter Disc, in the importation of music recordings from the United States (Moran 1998). The television company was engaged in the pan-European broadcasting of concerts of music stars such as Tina Turner and Pink Floyd. Early television programme sales were in entertainment and special events, particularly music and youth affairs. Crucially, IDTV entered a format exchange arrangement with US game show producer Ralph Andrews, benefiting especially from the latter's format for *Lingo*.

Located in central Amsterdam, IDTV has no production studios. Instead, it films on location or uses the facilities of a broadcaster. Through a series of subsidiary companies, the group also maintains a management agency, a theatre business, music interests as well as a film documentary unit. A subsidiary company, IDRA, was established in 1989 to formalize the format link with Ralph Andrews, who was subsequently bought out. IDRA survives as the international format licensing arm of the company.

IDTV has pursued a parallel path of international associations. IDTV has a small production branch in Belgium which has produced adaptations of game shows such as *Lingo* and 'reality' programmes such as *Taxi* for the Flemish commercial broadcasters. IDtv also has an agent in Spain in the shape of the production company Videozapping. Elsewhere, it licenses formats in its catalogue, maintaining a series of reciprocal first-look agreements with companies such as Beyond International in Australia (Borglund 2002).

Andrews sold IDTV the international rights to *Lingo* and this has proved to be the cash cow on which the company's format catalogue is founded. It sold a Dutch version to public broadcaster Vera which is still in production as are nine other versions in countries such as Sweden, Italy and France. Altogether over 25 adaptations have been licenced including productions as far afield as Israel and Malaysia. IDTV has over 50 formats available for licensing that have been devised in-house or acquired. Among the former are the game shows, *Trivial Pursuits* and *Boggle*, as well as several 'reality' formats such as *Taxi* and *A Matter of Life and Death*.

King World International

Illustrating the variety of kinds of companies that are active in the field of TV programme formats, King World has principally been a distributor. The company was founded in 1974 by Roger King. It began life as a distributor and its big break came in 1983 when it gained the syndication rights to *Wheel of Fortune* (Moran 1998). The company was controlled by the King family until a merger with CBS in January 2000. That merger produced CBS Enterprises, a division of CBS Broadcasting, Inc. The division encompasses King World Productions, Inc., the domestic syndication arm, and CBS Broadcast International, the worldwide television distribution unit, as well as King World Media Sales and CBS Consumer Products. While King World is not a devisor or developer of new formats, nevertheless it is heavily engaged in the worldwide production of its game show, reality and talk formats. These include *The Vault, Casino, Pictionary, Wheel of Fortune, Jeopardy, Hollywood Squares* and *Kids Say The Darndest Things.*

Planet 24/Castaway/Strix

The story of this group began in 1987 with the format of what later became known as *Expedition Robinson/Survivor* (Strix 2003; Brenton and Cohen 2003). As mentioned in Chapter 3 above, the format was the brainchild of UK-based Charlie Parsons. Originally, it was conceived as a kind of docu-soap on a desert island. Parsons worked in the United States in 1992 and took the format with him, continuing to work on its development. He also set up the company Planet 24 with partner Waheed Alli. By 1995, the format was complete and ready for production. However, Planet 24 could not gain a licensing agreement on either side of the Atlantic (Strix 2003). Under the title *Expedition Robinson*, the format was produced in Sweden in 1997. In turn, a US producer, Mark Burnett, reached an agreement with Parsons and persuaded US network CBS to commission a US version of the format (Burnett 2001). With the permission of the format owner, the original was changed extensively and under the title *Survivor* went to air. And while *Expedition Robinson* had done reasonably well in versions produced for Sweden and Germany, it was the US success of *Survivor* that turned the format into a very hot property. In turn, Planet 24 went on to produce *The Big Breakfast* and *The Word* for the UK marketplace.

Meanwhile, Parsons, Ali and a third partner, Bob Geldof sold Planet 24 to Carlton Communications PLC in 1999. In its stead, they set up Castaway Productions which held on to the format rights and continues to produce subsequent versions of *Survivor* in different territories across the world.

At the same time, Strix, the original producer of *Expedition Robinson/Survivor* in Sweden, continues its own engagement with reality television (Strix 2003). The company was set up in 1988 and its success with the Parsons' format has helped make it the largest production company in the Nordic countries. Since 1997, Strix has produced adaptations of the format for an escalating number of countries - Sweden, Denmark, Norway, Russia, the Netherlands, Belgium, Germany, Austria and the Baltic States. In addition, the company's knowledge and expertise expressed in this format has been sold for Robinson productions in Italy, Spain, Argentina and France. More recently, it has generated several successful in-house TV and Internet formats, the most famous of these being *The Bar*. Other formats created by Strix include *Harem, 360 Degrees, Solidarity, The Last Resort, The Farm, Wannabe* and *Ulla Medusa*. To date, it has licensed these and others in over 40 different countries across the world.

Screentime

This company was established by the coming together of two television executives - Des Monaghan had a background both in production and management while Bob Campbell had mostly been involved in the latter (Campbell 2003). The two had worked together at the Seven Network in Australia since 1988 and set up Screentime in 1996. The company now has branches in Australia, New Zealand, the United Kingdom and Ireland. It is a generalist company with interests in production, programme distribution, and format development and distribution. Until recently, its efforts were concentrated on the Australian and New Zealand markets. Drama series, mini series, telemovies, children's series, documentaries, infotainments and low budget 'reality' series have all figured among its output.

However, it was the company's acquisition of the format for *Pop Stars* that was to make Screentime an international player in the arena of formats. The latter had initially been developed as a low-key documentary series by a New Zealand film-maker. Screentime, though, recognized the concept's potential for promotion and merchandising and subsequently acquired it. The format was revamped as *Pop Stars* and the success of the first adaptation in Australia led to its remaking in over 40 different territories across the world. By this time, Monaghan had become the company's travelling consultant producer on this and other company formats including *Strip Search*.

In turn, the international distribution of its programmes and formats led Screentime to enter into its first joint venture agreement. In Ireland, the company had licensed local company *Shinawal*, headed by music entrepreneur, Larry Bass, to produce the series for RTE so that in 2002 a more long-term arrangement came into existence in the shape of *Screentime Shinawal*.

Taken together, these company outlines give some idea of the network of businesses that constitute the international programme format trade. As noted above, the listing is representative although it is far from exhaustive. A fuller catalogue of companies in different parts of the world is provided in Appendix iv. Commerce in TV programme formats is especially concentrated in Western Europe and the profiles have paid particular attention to the more important of these groups. However, besides markets, there are other structural dynamics in play that help constitute these disparate groups as a network. In the next chapter, I look at two major sets of linkage. These have to do with a format trade association on the one hand and the connections between the trade and business-format franchising on the other.

CHAPTER 8

Self-regulation and self-understanding

Formats have been 'circulating' in some form or other for 15 years now, but it is only in the last few years that we have seen a frenetic development of the format business. The combination of high production cost, high rating expectations, and audience demands for local heroes, have driven broadcasters to commission an increasing number of tried and tested programmes that are what we call 'formats' today.

Michele Rodrigue, CEO Distraction Formats (Interview Moran 2002)

The need for protection of Television Formats began with the creation of the first format. For many years Formats meant game shows and the market was small enough to be regulated amongst professional colleagues. In recent times the need for protection has escalated and disputes have increased.

Early FRAPA flyer (FRAPA 2000)

A trade association like FRAPA is only effective if its membership is universal among people operating in the business. I think that if someone stands outside of FRAPA, thumbs its nose at it, it might as well not be there. Our experience with FRAPA and Pop Idol was pretty unsatisfactory.

Bob Campbell, Screentime (2003)

Franchising as it is generally known today is a form of marketing or distribution in which a parent company grants an individual or a small company the right, or privilege, to do business in a prescribed manner over a certain period of time in a specified place.

Business Textbook (Vaughan 1979)

This chapter is concerned with continuing efforts by the trade to further formalize itself as a business. As is suggested below, charges of theft, legal disputes, costly court outcomes and so on imply that this is a Darwinian world of chaotic and destructive competition. Nonetheless, it is not always in companies' best business interests to act so aggressively. There are elements that unite as well as ones that move them apart. Trade fairs and the turnover of individuals often bring companies together. Additionally, as part of a general growth in the size and frequency of activity in the industry, efforts both to organize an effective trade association and the opportunity to locate the industry within larger parameters of the service industries are well worth looking at here. Hence, the chapter is divided into two parts having to do with the Format Registration And Protection Association (FRAPA) and franchising.

FRAPA and self-regulation

As this book has already suggested, the TV programme format distribution industry displays a characteristic feature of many areas of trade and commerce. This has to do with the fact that at certain times and situations companies are fiercely competitive rivals whereas in other circumstances they can act together in what is seen to be their common interest. This apparent contradiction is encountered again in the next chapter that has to do with copyright where the industry constantly behaves as though written formats attract copyright protection although some of the same organizations sometime choose to thumb their noses at this idea. In other words, there is a constant tension between the industry as a kind of club where particular rules of behaviour are in place and the notion of the industry as a barbaric arena with no holds barred. Perhaps a better way to put the same point is to notice that while the larger companies occasionally bruise each other, it is their capacity to maul and swallow smaller companies that has prompted the urge towards some kind of industry self regulation.

Looked at in this way, the development of FRAPA as an industry body appears to demonstrate a move from a perceived ad hoc stage of the format business to a more formal system of behaviour and control. As Michele Rodrigue from Distraction explained it, the move to form such a group was inevitable as the industry itself became larger:

> Because of the creative nature of the business, it rapidly became necessary to ensure that the great new ideas reached the screens. Therefore the industry created its own self-regulatory body, FRAPA (Format Recognition and Protection Association), whose members represent the vast majority of all format transactions worldwide. (Rodrigue 2002)

The organizational seeds of FRAPA lie in casual groupings of format owners and distributors coming together at such venues as MIPTV and MIPCOM. One such grouping was that informal network, mentioned in the previous chapter, which included Harry de Winter, IDtv, Joop van den Ende and Gestmusic. Such groupings existed not only for commercial purposes but also found it useful to share business information. In turn, in 1999, a group of UK terrestrial broadcasters decided to sign up to a voluntary code of practice designed to prevent the theft of production ideas. From here, it was only a short step to a proposal for a more international trade association, principally designed to attempt to safeguard formats without costly legal action (FRAPA 2000).

FRAPA was launched at MIPTV in 2000 when a group of television executives came together to discuss how to find a solution to format piracy. David Lyle, who was then Fremantle Media's entertainment president for North America, became head of FRAPA's steering committee and was a driving force in the Association's establishment. By MIPCOM in October that same year, an organization had taken shape and the FRAPA membership lists were opened. In February the following year, following the example of various literary registry services, FRAPA launched the world's first free International Television Paper Format Registry. Earlier, format owners had frequently 'registered' written formats by claiming copyright protection on them and depositing these with local industry organizations such as TV writers' associations.

Described as an unofficial patents' office, FRAPA now oversees the registration of paper formats. The process is intended to clearly document the point in time from which a certain TV idea has existed. The Association sees this kind of chronological registration as an important step on the way to solving disputes. In particular, the measure is seen as limiting the industry practice of pirating new formats if licensing negotiations fail. Finally, too, one other documentation service should be mentioned. This relates to FRAPA's website where it maintains an online archive of press clippings relating to format protection and disputes (FRAPA 2000).

In point of fact, the move to form an association was a propitious one coming as it did in the midst of a string of legal disputes over alleged format infringements. These copyright problems particularly affected different UK production companies. For instance, former Planet 24 boss Charlie Parsons was involved in a multi-million dollar legal wrangle over Endemol Entertainment's hit *Big Brother*. The previous year, Celador had successfully blocked transmission of a Danish show that the company claimed was a copy of the *Who Wants to be a Millionaire?* format. Additionally, in 1998/9 Hat Trick Productions was in dispute with the Australian ABC over the latter's *Good News Week*, claiming that this programme copied their format for *Have I Got News For You*. Although these matters were resolved, nevertheless the incidence of these, and several other battles underlined the on-going need for another means of resolving disputes, perhaps by a mechanism made available through a trade association.

FRAPA membership is open to organizations and companies operating in the areas of television broadcasting and programme production. The aim is to persuade major producers and broadcasters involved in the area to join as well as encouraging legal officers to also participate. The Association has attracted many of the most important format companies in the international trade. Among the initial members were Pearson (now Fremantlemedia), GMG Endemol, Columbia TriStar, King World, Distraction, Mentorn International, Hat Trick Productions, Celador and Expand Images. Nonetheless, over the past four or five years, the reported number of members appears to have fluctuated considerably, varying from as few as 20 to as many as 100 (FRAPA 2000; Kingsley 2003).

To put this another way, one might suggest that although FRAPA has been broadly successful in signing many of the larger US/UK/Western European companies that feel they belong to the format 'club', nevertheless companies elsewhere have elected not to join. Indeed, given the fact that there are probably television production companies involved in adaptation in other parts of the world, including, for instance, India and PR China, that have never attended the international trade fairs and have probably never heard of FRAPA, then, it would appear that this body has quite some distance to go in terms of achieving some of its objectives.

FRAPA's general aim is to promote to producers, broadcasters and the law the concept of formats as unique, intellectual properties. Thanks to the generosity of North Rhine Westphalia's permanent state secretary, an office has been established in Cologne in Germany headed up by attorney Christoph Fey. His long-term goal for the organization is reported to be to establish an environment where formats are respected by the industry and acknowledged by law (NRW/FRAPA).

Recognizing that legal outcomes of format disputes in different jurisdictions are often unpredictable, generally frustrating and extremely expensive, FRAPA's first aim has been to act to mediate and arbitrate disputes outside the court system.

In its first two-and-a-half years, FRAPA was said to be involved in eight to ten cases of dispute. However, the hopes regarding arbitration seem not to have worked out. This is a binding process in law and company lawyers did not want to lose control of cases to a panel. Instead, the emphasis has been on non-binding mediation. FRAPA offers a confidential service that may be useful in dispute resolution. Because the groups involved may be conducting business together in the near future, non-binding mediation does not threaten these relationships (FRAPA 2003).

FRAPA's long-term objective is to put pressure on governments worldwide to create clearer copyright laws including campaigning to have TV programme formats protected as intellectual property. This includes shaping the way online formats are developed and protected. However, Fey admits that obtaining recognition for formats in law may be a long process as case books in Europe do not offer many precedents. On the other hand, cases in jurisdictions further afield such as the United States and India appear to offer more promise (NRW/FRAPA).

FRAPA has now been in existence for six years and it is worth summarizing its achievements as well as its problems. First, it has signed up at least some of the important producers and broadcasters in the format trade even if many others have remained outside the organization. Lack of industry membership makes it difficult for FRAPA to function as an effective alternative to the law as a means of resolving disputes. In any case, it is very difficult for any trade association to also act as policeman in disputes between some of its members. Decisions in disputes will, inevitably, have the effect of creating a schism. Finally, too, FRAPA's long-term goal of promoting TV programme formats to government as intellectual property also seems to need to travel a further distance before it might issue in any legislative success.

On the other side of the ledger, it should be admitted that FRAPA does mark an important stage in the development of the format trade. It offers members a useful trade association. It has succeeded in attracting the loyalty of a healthy number of members. And finally it is an important step forward in terms of the industry gaining a greater knowledge of what in fact it is about. The second half of the chapter follows this point by looking at yet another context in which the trade might be situated as a means of clarifying just what kind of industry it actually is.

Franchising

In Chapter 2, I suggested in passing that the notion of the format developed in the business-format franchising industry was very relevant to our attempt to develop a satisfactory understanding of the notion of the TV programme format. In the remainder of this chapter, I return to this link to further probe the nature of the business that is TV programme format distribution. What light, then, does a knowledge of franchising throw on TV programme format exchange?

First, one should be clear what the label format does not mean. The term is currently gaining favour as a means of labelling contemporary developments in television. Hence, for instance, executive producer Paul Jackson at Fremantlemedia has recently described a television series that recycles some of the characters from the long running series *The Bill* as a franchise. Equally, TV journalists are more and more given to categorizing the several programmes versions derived from US series such as *Law and Order* and *CSI* as franchises. Obviously, there is nothing wrong with such usage. Equally, there is nothing particularly illuminating about this either. The term franchising here simply means a spin-off, remake or reversioning of elements drawn from an original to produce an adaptation.

In fact, though, the term may possibly be more productive than this. It deserves more careful application in relation to TV programme formats. A glance at the history of the word helps one to understand links between the TV format industry and the franchising industry.

Franchising is a business arrangement that concerns the area of distribution of goods and services (Vaughan 1979). This operation has a history of nearly 200 years. The term franchise itself goes back many centuries and means the granting of a right. Although first used in relation to matters of state, the term has been used in connection with commerce from the Middle Ages onwards. Here, to franchise means to invest with a privilege. In the twentieth century, the term's meaning expanded to include a method of business distribution and the word seems to have entered common useage in the West from the 1950s onwards (Dicke 1982).

In fact, authors writing about franchising as a business operation note that this kind of arrangement has a history spanning at least two centuries. It is common to distinguish between two kinds of franchising (Coltman 1988). The first, the older and more common type, is that of product franchising. This has to do with the business relationship between two parties where the second acts as a distributing agent or dealer, helping to circulate a product or other tangible good. Several types of product franchising come to mind including car dealerships and petrol franchising. This type is well over 100 years old and, although capable of various reconfigurations, shows no signs of weakening its hold in the world of business commerce.

Meanwhile, a second type, more relevant to the business of TV programme format exchange, is more recent. This is the business-format franchise. It has been explained as follows: 'The franchiser licenses a business format, operating system and trademark together with a comprehensive package of services to its franchisee and may or may not sell tangible products to them' (Vaughan 1979). Examples of this second type include fast food restaurants, convenience stores, car rentals and motels. Clearly, all of these businesses are location-based so that one part of the services offered by the franchisor to a would-be franchisee is that of experienced assistance in helping to locate an outlet where the public will be offered the particular set of products or services licensed from the franchisor by the licensee.

Given these different dates, it is worth recalling the sketchy history of the TV format business already mentioned above. As was noticed, there are many precedents for the practice of television programme copying to be found in the history of the media in the redeployment of successful book, newspaper and magazine formulas in different places. Equally, the story of, first, radio broadcasting and then early television is also littered with many examples of programme adaptation. Hence, for instance, from the late 1930s onwards, in radio, first, and then in television, there have been many examples of programmes being imitated from place to place and from time to time, not forgetting that very many radio programmes were also adapted to television. However, for the most part, these remakes were sporadic in frequency and restricted in their national and international appearance. Even where programme owners were aware that copying was occurring, this tended to be without the owner playing any kind of active role in the redeployment of the programme formula.

Notwithstanding this kind of tendency, one can suggested that the actual roots of the TV programme format industry are probably to be found in the 1950s and were, in all likelihood, inspired by the same forces that were affecting the emergence of business-format franchising. In effect, just as their business colleagues in other service industries were conceiving of a new form of distribution, so some TV programme owners and producers were more clear-headed about the potential business opportunities involved in facilitating TV programme remaking. After all, incidental copying or imitation was one thing. Systematically facilitating programme adaptation was something else, a new business departure. Thus, the earliest example that I am aware of of this conscious packaging of elements for the methodical adaptation of a programme, concerns the example of the children's television programme *Romper Room*, that has already been mentioned. This programme first appeared on a local US television station in Baltimore in 1953.

Although the Baltimore version of the *Romper Room* programme was reasonably successful, its creators - husband and wife team, Bert and Nancy Claster - turned down a CBS Network's offer to buy the programme for network broadcast. Instead, the Clasters hired the format to a string of local television stations across the country. Those that signed up with the Claster's company to use the formula to make their own version of the programme received the rights to use their own hostess and to obtain merchandise and materials representing the programme including a grinning jack-in-the-box holding a stake with the series title and Mr Do Be, a smiling yellow jacket. Episodes were loosely structured to consist of games, book readings and other activities using a range of *Romper Room* products. As part of the franchising arrangement, Nancy Claster, who had been the original on-air hostess in Baltimore, ran weeklong courses for college-graduate hostesses who would front the programme. By 1957, 22 stations in the US were taking the format. Six years later, 119 US stations had their own *Romper Room*, each led by a college graduate hostess. By then, too, the format was being distributed internationally and included several versions being made in Australia and in Japan.

In other words, coincident with or perhaps part of the development of a new kind of franchising, that of the business-format, TV programme format distribution shows some of its earliest signs of emergence in the postwar period. Hence, in the future, 1953 may come to be recognized as a key date that saw not only the establishment of new fast food restaurant franchising including those of Burger King, Kentucky Fried Chicken and McDonald's but also saw the franchising of *Romper Room* as a harbinger of the TV programme format industry that was to come. Be that as it may, the copying of TV programmes - both authorized and unauthorized - has continued down to the present. However, for the most part, the different knowledges accumulated by the original producers remained scattered and undocumented. Instead, a format had to be inferred from the residual traces available in broadcast episodes of the programme and, with fiction, from scripts. By contrast, it has only been in the recent present (some date the change to around 1990) that producers have begun to follow the example of the clusters with *Romper Room* and systematize and document various production knowledges that come together under the name of the format.

Taking this as a cue, one can note that every TV programme, like every other kind of artefact, is capable of being adapted, imitated or copied. However, format is the name that the trade gives to the deliberate enhancement of the adaptability of a programme. In other words, a TV programme format is that set of interconnected industry knowledges having to do not only with production but with finance, marketing, broadcasting and other areas, consciously assembled, with a view to facilitating and increasing the adaptability of the programme. As a business service, the TV programme format industry can be seen to be a branch of a larger industry, namely that of franchising, most especially that of business-format franchising. Whether one believes TV programme formats to be a new, distinct type, following on from product franchising and service franchising, or an extension of the second type, the fact remains that knowing more about the general business of franchising will help one understand more clearly the peculiar business that is TV programme format distribution.

Continuities and differences

Recognizing the TV programme format business as a branch of a larger franchising operation needs further commentary. Distribution of the format is the key operation and, piracy apart, this always occurs under a licensing agreement. This, in turn, means that the two parties should be recognized as the licensor and the licensee, respectively, with the licensing contract being the element that binds them together.

Sometimes, as we have seen, there is a variation on this relationship with the two parties being one and the same. However, this kind of O&O operation with the branch being owned and operated by the parent company is familiar enough in other areas of business-format franchising. So, too, one can see the production outlets of Endemol and Fremantlemedia in particular territories as not only motivated by a desire to maximize profit but also as part of a larger tendency within franchising industries.

Several commentators writing about franchising have noted that licensor and licensee have tended to differ so far as their relative power within the market is concerned (Vaughan 1979; Dicke 1982; Coltman 1988). Format licensors tend to belong to the world of big (international) business whereas many licensees can be characterized as small (national) businesses. The latter arena is frequently marked by high rates of product and business failures. Clearly, one of the general effects of TV formats, like business-format franchising in general, is to help stabilize and organize production and broadcasting industries at this latter end of the spectrum.

Another continuity between TV programme format distribution and business-format franchising is the fact that licensor and licensee are in different businesses. The licensee's trade is that of programme production and broadcast where the market is the combined figure of the viewer and the advertiser. On the other hand, the licensor is only incidentally engaged in the business of television production and broadcast. Television provides the circumstance or pretext for the business transaction. Agent Ben Silverman is drawing attention to this reality when he remarks that he is, 'a miner for highend intellectual property. ... The fact that it manifests itself in the dimension of television tends to add the kitsch value' (Goldsmith 2001). Put this way, the TV programme format distributor has more in common with, say, the McDonald's company than with other agencies within the television industry.

However, while passing tips on about making a TV programme may have something in common with hamburgerology, finally these are quite dissimilar businesses. There are several important variations that make TV programme format distribution different to that of business-format franchising. One obvious point of departure is the fact that the licensee in this case is not involved in any services equivalent to choosing outlets for licensees. In addition, as has been repeatedly mentioned, unauthorized adaptation of programmes is very common across many territories worldwide.

There also appears to be at least two further differences that are much more important. Brands are the first of these. More particularly, what is important is the relative power of brands in the area of business-format franchising and that of TV programme format distribution. If a brand is thought of as the kind of commercial and cultural aura or buzz that surrounds a name, whether it be that of a company such as the BBC or a programme such as *Who Wants to be a Millionaire?*, then it is the case that, to date at least, no TV programme format appears to have the brand power of companies operating in the area of business-format franchising (Todreas 1999; Bellamy, Robert and Trott 2000; Walker 2001; Rodgers, Epstein and Reeves 2002).

Secondly, there is the fact that, generally speaking, the service that is licensed - the TV programme format - usually has a much shorter shelf life than many other services in the field of business-format franchising. Hence, contracts binding licensor and licensee tend to have a much shorter duration than those operating in business franchising where a standard contract can be as short as twenty years and as long as a lifetime (Vaughan 1979). With TV programme format licensing contracts on the other hand, even a highly successful 'reality' series such as *Big Brother* only results in a limited number of episodes so that the contract on a particular series soon comes to an end.

All the same three further comments should be added. First, the fact that the move in 2004 by RTL in Germany to have Endemol continue the most recent German series of *Big Brother* as a daily, continuing programme suggests a move to at least test whether licensed formats may have longer shelf lives than is currently the case. More importantly, though, may be the fact that contracts concerning a single format are less significant than those between format catalogue owners and local broadcasters and producers under such arrangements as joint venture agreements. Finally, there is the point that the form of franchising involved in TV programme formats may, in fact, still be evolving.

Take, for instance, the matter of cross-platforming and technological convergence. The big issue to date is that it has not been revenue generating but rather a value adding service to the programme aired on TV (Glori 2002; Anon. 2003). There seems to be significant potential for TV type formats to be converted into online gaming and data monitoring experiences initially connected with programme format but soon bypassing any on-air programme (Anon. 2003). In what may be a key aspect of cross-platform synergizing across media to maximize economic viability and conceptual productivity, Endemol's experience with *The Big Diet*, mentioned in the last chapter, is highly relevant to such a supposition.

Put another way, the TV programme format industry is still evolving both at a market level and in terms of general understanding. The investigation up to this point has been principally crouched in terms whereby the trade makes sense of itself. In the remainder of the book, I change focus and look at the area from the point of view of legal definition and practice. And indeed, the point of departure is the fact that the industry behaves as though formats are legally protected whereas those trained in the law are less than certain of such a proposition.

CHAPTER 9

The law regarding TV formats

Justin Malbon

In terms of originating formats, the real problem is less about coming up with ideas and more about protecting them: Intellectual property is easy to steal. While we were negotiating The Bar for Germany, another broadcaster was involved in the negotiations and when they lost, they immediately started with another production company to make a rip off, and they set up a club instead of a bar. That's what's happening all over. (Kingsley 2003)

There is no recognized legal category known as 'format' rights. It is, as we have seen, an industry term that tends these days to refer to game shows and 'reality shows'. Although the law does not protect a format in itself, a degree of legal protection is gained by deploying a range of legal rights, including copyright, confidentiality, passing off, trademarks and design protection. The savvy format creator or producer will enlist these rights to the greatest effect possible to fend off copycats. Producers also need to be aware of these rights to avoid being sued by format creators, broadcasters and other format producers.

Before venturing into a discussion about the laws that can be harnessed to protect a format, we will consider the various situations in which you, as either a creator of TV formats, a writer, producer or broadcaster, would become interested in protecting a format or avoiding breaching the rights relating to another existing format. Given that there are so many players involved in the creation and production of a formatted TV series, we will simplify things by taking the point of view of the producer. The producer is engaged at all stages of production; from when a format proposal is first pitched to the producer, to its development into something more than a broad proposal, to pre-production, production and then on-licensing the programme to a broadcaster in a home and overseas territories.

There are innumerable variations on the model in which a creator pitches a format proposal to a producer who then proceeds to develop the show, find the finance and have it produced. The producer, for example, might simply purchase the license of a proven success in another territory and produce it in his/her home territory; or the creator themself might become the producer. Or the producer might simply develop the concept to a certain level of refinement and then offer it to a distributor, who will then seek out broadcasters to produce the show.

Freda pitches her project

We will take an imaginary programme called *Player Challenge*, which its creator, Freda Lyons, pitches to you. You are a producer at the production house NewFormat Productions. We will follow the story from producer's point of view, moving from the pitch, to development, production and broadcast; all the while watching out for hidden legal snares and making use of legal rights and protections.

We begin with Freda pitching her proposal to you in your office, or maybe at Hugo's Coffee House, where the coffee is great and the background noise does not distract you from hearing Freda out. Freda comes across as outgoing, creative and very enthusiastic about her proposal. Her proposal, you tell her, has promise. You both agree that you will take her proposal back to your company, NewFormats, and get a sense of the company's level of interest in the project. You agree to get back to her within the next couple of weeks.

Now for the legal part: the first question is whether Freda has copyright in the proposal she pitched to you, and the second question is whether you are under an obligation to keep the proposal confidential. We will deal with the copyright issue first.

Does Freda have copyright in her proposal?

First rule of thumb: no copyright in ideas

The first rule of thumb is that Freda will only have copyright in the material that exists in a tangible form. As I type this paragraph into my computer, I gain copyright in what I have written. The moment ideas take tangible form, whether typed into a computer, written on a page or dictated into a recording machine, it automatically gains copyright, and there is no requirement to register the copyright. Registration is possible in some countries including the United States. Registration does not grant copyright, but may offer some strategic advantages in protecting copyright, as we mention later in this chapter in the section headed 'Is it necessary to register copyright?' If Freda merely discusses the proposal with you, and does not have the matters she is discussing existing in any tangible form, whether on paper or on a computer disc or hard drive, or as a videotape, or voice tape or other form of recording, then she has no copyright merely in her ideas.

Second rule of thumb: the work must be original

The second rule of thumb is that a work must be an 'original' work. It does not take a great deal of originality to meet this legal criterion. So long as the work is not a substantial copy of another copyright work, and involved at least some degree of thought (as opposed to mindless copying from another source, including a direct copying of a non-copyright work like a Dickens' novel), then the law will treat it as an original work. We discuss the originality requirement later in this chapter under the heading 'What's original?' Nor will Freda have copyright in any broad 'genre' elements themselves that are contained in her proposal. She may, however, be able to gain copyright in if she combines the collection of genre elements in an original way within a recognizable and original structure.

Copyright law does not protect a genre, type, and style because their scope is too broad, and providing them protection would greatly hamper creativity. As to precisely what elements of storytelling, music and format shows constitute a genre is a moot point. Some elements are obviously a genre: there is no copyright in a 'game show', 'quiz show' or 'reality show' in itself. That is, even if, you were transported back in time and became the first person to come up with the idea of a game show and proceeded to produce one, you will not have copyright in something as general as the idea of having a game show on TV. Just as the creators of *Survivor*, who believed they had developed a new concept in reality shows (which they probably did), could not gain copyright in something as broad as a reality show.

The distinction between a genre (which cannot gain copyright) and an original work (which has copyright) is fairly obvious at the extreme ends of the scale, but becomes increasingly uncertain and blurred as we move towards the centre point of these extremes. At the extreme end of the scale it can be said that there is no copyright in the idea of a horror movie, a thriller, a comedy and so on. If you write a comedy, no one is going to sue you for breach of copyright just because you wrote a comedy. Even if you write a comedy script in which a boy meets a girl, and despite many misunderstandings and much bumbling, eventually fall in love, you will not be infringing the copyright of other boy meets girl comedies simply because you have these primary elements. But if you have a script about a character called Barry Egan who has seven sisters, runs a toilet-plunger vender wholesale business, is a social misfit who begins to fall in love with Lena Leonard and gets mixed up with some bad people who want to extort money from Barry after he phoned their business for phone sex, and let's say you call that script *Punch-Drunk Love* - then you may have problems. Paul Thomas Anderson has already written that script, along with the equally idiosyncratic *Magnolia* and *Boogie Nights*.

Somewhere between writing what might generically be called a boy meets girl comedy and the script for *Punch-Drunk Love* lays the grey area of copyright law. Numerous attempts have been made by judges and legal commentators to establish tests to remove the grey from the grey areas, with varying success. US Supreme Court Judge Learned Hand famously proposed the 'abstractions test':

> *Upon any work, and especially upon a play, a great number of patterns of increasing generality will fit equally well, as more and more of the incident is left out. The last may perhaps be no more than the most general statement of what the play is about, and at times might consist of only its title; but there is a point in this series of abstractions where they are no longer protected, since otherwise the playwright could prevent the use of his 'ideas', to which, parts from their expression, his property is never extended.* (*Nicols* v. *Universal Pictures Corp.* (1930:121))

Basically, the judge was saying that at some point between the more abstract, generalized descriptions and elements of a play and the particular play with its unique characters and plot lays the point at which copyright kicks in. Not an overly precise test, admittedly, but it does serve to emphasize that greater particularity brings with it a greater probability of copyright protection. As another judge said, somewhat tongue in cheek, the law of copyright is built on two axioms: '(1) copyright protection covers only the expression of ideas and not ideas themselves; and (2) the first axiom is more of an amorphous characterisation than it is a principled guidepost' (*Chuck Blore and Don Richman Inc.* v. *20/20 Advertising* (1987)).

Suffice to say at this point, there is no neat mechanical way of deciding whether there is copyright infringement when we enter the grey area between a literal copying of a copyright work (which will obviously be an infringement of copyright) and a copying of a number of stylistic, genre and general type elements of an existing copyright work. Invariably, formats reside in this grey area. Because of the significance of this issue for formats, we will give the matter closer consideration in the next chapter.

Third rule of thumb: copyright applies to more than literal copying

The discussion about *Punch-Drunk Love* hints at a third rule of thumb, which is that copyright protection of Freda's work extends beyond a literal copying of her work. That is, if you took her treatment or detailed outline of the TV series, and simply changed a few words here and there and rearranged the ordering of her sentences, but kept the essence of her treatment or outline the same, you may well be infringing her copyright; and she could successfully sue. But the precise point at which variations from her literal text would avoid infringement is imprecise. Returning to *Punch-Drunk Love* as a completed script, we can see that it sets out an elaborate and detailed story. The literal text of the script is obviously protected by copyright. If we take one-step back from the literal text and have the same characters doing and saying more or less the same things as in *Punch-Drunk Love*, we may well still have copyright protection. But as we step further back and copy only the more general elements of the script, there is less likelihood that *Punch-Drunk Love* scriptwriter Paul Thomas Anderson will be able to successfully claim copyright over an allegedly copycat story. He is unlikely to be able to successfully sue over another story that is simply about a neurotic American man who runs a business and despite the odds falls in love with a beautiful English woman who understands and engages with his somewhat eccentric understandings of love and romance. So long as the names of the characters in the other story are different, along with other plot and character elements, then at some point there is little or no chance in succeeding in a copyright action.

As another example, taking the case of *Who Wants to be a Millionaire?* there is no copyright in the concept of a show in which a host asks ordinary people questions, with prizes going to the contestants who provide correct answers. At this level of generality, the law offers no protection because it is too broad a concept. But if we take the combination of the title to the TV quiz show, add the particular set design, the lighting, the music, the particular one on one nature of the relationship between the quiz show host and the guest being quizzed and the rules of the game that apply, then we have something unique, even if the particular questions being asked and the guests change with each programme. Whether this unique combination of elements can be protected by the law of copyright or not is not completely settled by the law; but the increasing likelihood is that it is capable of protection.

Copyright provides the holder with an exclusive right to reproduce the work in a material form and to produce an adaptation of the work. Copyright is not limited to pitch documents, the production bible or (possibly) the dramatic performance of the show; it can also apply to any compilations of questions for a quiz show, or the creation any other compilation of information, or the creation of a computer database of information for the show. Rights may also attach to the creation of computer programmes for the show.

In summary, if Freda simply presents you with a verbal outline of her format idea, and does not provide you anything in written, video or other tangible form, then she will have no copyright in what she has told you. You are free to take all her ideas and make them your own without infringing copyright. Freda might claim, however, that you breached the confidentiality in which she presented her ideas to you - which we will deal later in this chapter.

If Freda has presented you material in a tangible form, the question then becomes whether she has moved beyond simply serving up fairly common-place genre elements, or whether she has created an 'original' work. We will consider what the law means by originality in terms of copyright next. The more elaborated and detailed her pitch documents are, the more likely she will be able to gain copyright in them. Broadly speaking, in deciding whether there is copyright, the questions to be asked are:

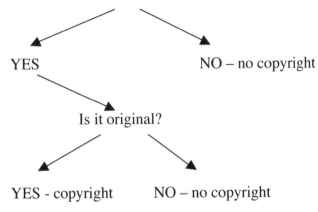

Is the 'format' expressed in some tangible form?

YES   NO – no copyright

Is it original?

YES - copyright   NO – no copyright

Fig. 9.1 - Flowchart - is the format in a tangible form?

What's original?

The law does not require a particularly high standard of originality for a work to gain copyright. The work does not have to be particularly creative or novel. It simply needs to be the work of the author and not a substantial copy of another work. There is some disagreement amongst various courts throughout the world as to the minimum degree of creativity required. The US Supreme Court has said that there must be some creative or aesthetic to the work to gain copyright; 'there must be an investment of at least "modicum of creativity" for it to be original' (*Feist Publications Inc.* v. *Rural Telephone Service Co. Inc.* (1991)). An Australian court disagrees saying that the law merely requires originality and not creativity. The British House of Lords, on the other hand says, 'to constitute an original work, the author must have exercised "knowledge, skill, labour and judgement"' (*Cramp* v. *Smythson* (1944)). French law requires that the work must bear the 'imprint of the personality of the author', and German law requires that the work requires personal intellectual input for it to be original. It seems then that a monkey hitting keys randomly on a computer keyboard is incapable of gaining copyright in the text it produces.

The problem of copyright for formats

Particular problems arise with format shows regarding copyright because they invariably make heavy use of genre elements, and lack detailed scripts with plot lines and characters as normally understood in terms of comedies and dramas. There are a number of legal cases, particularly in the United Kingdom and Germany, that illustrate the courts' reluctance to find there is copyright in a format - even if the format exists as a completed TV series. There are, however, other cases that suggest courts are increasingly likely to find copyright existing in format shows, and that anyone who substantially copies the show will be found to have infringed copyright. If there is an infringement, a court could order compensation (known in law as 'damages') for the harmed party.

The way the law decides copyright issues in relation to format programmes will be discussed in the next chapter. Suffice to say at this point that Freda would be well advised to make her proposal as detailed as possible. A few other specific questions arise in relation to copyright, including whether it is necessary to register the copyright material and how long does the copyright last?

Is it necessary to register copyright?

There is no requirement for the author to register his or her work to gain copyright. In some countries like the United States there are advantages in registration, even though the author automatically gains copyright on creating the work. An author can get a stop order (injunction) from a court preventing the distribution or sale of a work that infringes your copyright, whether or not the work is registered. However, in the United States you can only gain monetary compensation (damages) for the infringement if your work is registered. Also, if there is a dispute about whose work was created first, a court will presume that the registered work was created at the time of registration. Registration requires sending an application to the US Register of Copyrights and payment of a small fee. Proof of registration follows about eight to twelve weeks later.

If you have copyright under the laws of the country in which you created your work, you will automatically gain copyright in the work in most countries throughout the world. This is because of an international agreement known as the Berne Convention for the Protection of Literary and Artistic Works to which most countries are signed up. Under the Berne Convention, if a work that has copyright in the country in which it is created, it will automatically gain copyright in all the other countries. This overcomes the problem that caused much angst for Charles Dickens. He unfortunately wrote his great works before any international agreement on copyright existed, which meant that his books were published in the United States without his consent and without him receiving any royalties. He had no copyright in his own work in the United States and most other countries.

Very few countries outside the United States have registration processes. This can lead to problems for authors who are at risk of having their work ripped-off by another party. One problem is proving the work was created before the copycat work was created. What is required is evidence of prior authorship. An author can either post the work to herself or himself in a registered sealed envelope and not open the envelope when it arrives. The author could point to the post-office's date stamp as independent evidence of the date on which the document was sent. Alternatively, the document could be sent to the author's lawyer or some other independent party who could note down the date of receiving the document. Another possibility for creators of format documentation (such as scripts, outlines and production bibles) who are members of the Format Protection and Recognition Association (FRAPA) is to send two copies of the documentation to FRAPA, who will retain one copy and time stamp and return the other (see http://www.frapa.org). Creators should also add the © symbol together with the year of copyright to his or her work, which might have the effect of warning off potential infringers.

As we know, the author of a work gains copyright in his or her work. If there is more than one author, then each gains copyright in the work. It is possible for different authors to gain separate copyright in different sections of the work they solely write. If authors wish to claim separate copyright it is wise to clearly claim authorship from the outset. The published work should clearly state that part A is authored by Georgina, part B by Harry and so on. As we have mentioned previously, an author can assign their copyright to someone else so that the purchaser of the copyright gains all the rights of the author. Alternatively, the author can retain copyright, but provide a license to another person to use the work.

How long does copyright last?
In many countries copyright lasts for the life of the author, plus 50 years after their death. This means that whoever is named in the author's will gains all the rights and the royalties, unless the author sold them off before they died. Europe and the United States apply life plus 70 years, with an increasing number of countries also adopting that period. If the author assigns (sells) their copyright to another party, the other party holds the copyright for the period the author would have held it if they had not sold the rights.

Moral rights
Included in the cluster of intellectual property rights is the 'moral rights' of the creator. This right derives from French law, which recognizes the creator's *droit moral* in their work. A number of other countries recognize this right, by either adopting or making modifications to the French model. If the law grants creators moral rights, it usually entitles them to a right to the 'integrity' of their work, and a right to be credited for their work, that is an attribution right. The moral right usually lasts as long as the underlying copyright. In some countries the creator cannot assign their moral right, but they may be able to waive (that is in effect, ignore) their right. The integrity right protects the creator from having their work mutilated or distorted in a way that would harm their honour or reputation. So if you were a renowned screenwriter and wrote a drama in which you dealt with the issue of religious intolerance in a nuanced and sympathetic way, but after the sale of your script the director turns it into a jingoistic rant against followers of non-

Christian faiths, then this might damage your reputation and harm the integrity of your work.

In deciding whether the integrity of your work has been infringed a court will apply a subjective and objective test. The subjective test requires finding out whether the creator believes their work has been used in a way that prejudices their honour or reputation. If this is so, the court proceeds to the objective test, and asks experts whether in their opinion reputation harm has been done. There must be a positive response to both tests before the court will find infringement. The attribution right means that you are to be credited as the author or creator of your work, regardless of the fact that you have assigned your copyright to someone else.

Freda options her project

Assume then that you believe that Freda's proposal for her format *Player Challenge* has a real possibility of becoming a commercial success. If you also believe that her proposal is sufficiently detailed and original to attract copyright protection, you will eventually need to obtain the right from her to use her copyright and other interests in the project to proceed with production. At this early stage you might not have the funds to buy out all her rights without first obtaining backing from an investor, broadcaster or distributor. What you might then propose is that Freda sign an option agreement. Typically, the agreement would offer Freda a relatively low sum of money, a few hundred dollars or pounds, for her agreement not to sell the rights to anyone else for the period of the option. Option agreements are usually for between six to eighteen months, with a right of renewal (after payment of a further fee) for an additional six to twelve months.

Many option agreements will also have attached to it a purchase of copyright agreement. The option agreement will state that the parties agree to enter into the attached purchase agreement if the producer elects during the option period to purchase the copyright from the creator. The purchase agreement will offer a substantially greater sum of money to the creator for the outright sale of the copyright and all other associated rights to the producer. In some countries a purchase agreement is called an assignment of copyright agreement, which simply means the creator passes all their rights over to the producer for an agreed amount of money, and for an appropriate credit in the opening or closing credits (or both) to the finished TV show.

Freda assigns her copyright

You may have gathered by now that copyright is an important legal right. The owner of the copyright can prevent unauthorized copying - that is, infringement - of their work. And as we have seen, the creator, Freda, can option her scripts and other copyright material to a producer for a fee, and eventually sell and transfer (assign) her copyright to the producer for an even higher amount. The producer of a TV show (let us say, a drama series) who holds the copyright to the series can grant a license to broadcasters for a fee to broadcast the show.

This book does not attempt to deal with the law regarding the production of a TV episode. The law applying to the production of a TV drama or comedy is much the same as that applying to a TV format show. We will briefly canvass some of the relevant legal issues regarding format shows in the remainder of the chapter. Further information on legal aspects of TV production can be found in numerous legal guides and books. As we have mentioned, different issues do arise, however, regarding the likelihood of copyright protection for a format show. There is a deal of legal controversy as to whether a format is capable of gaining copyright. This controversy is further discussed in the next chapter. In the absence of copyright, other legal strategies can be deployed to offer some protection against copycats. These include having the title to the show trademarked, suing the copycat for anti-competitive conduct (including suing for passing off), designs and patents.

Keeping it confidential

Even if Freda does not have much, or indeed anything, in writing or some other tangible form when she pitches her project, she might nevertheless be able to claim that the information she gave you was given on a confidential basis. If this is so, and you use that information in a way that causes her loss (for example, you proceed to make a TV series and cut her out of any earnings) then she may be able to successfully sue you for her loss.

There are a number of factors a court takes into account when deciding whether the information was given in confidence. A court takes into account any evidence that players in the television industry consider a pitch session as a circumstance in which commercially valuable information is likely to be passed on and would normally be treated confidentially. Also, if Freda did provide any documents or e-mails in which she stated that the material was confidential or the meeting was held on a confidential basis - that would also support Freda's case. It does not matter, in itself, that any material given to you lacked copyright protection. However, Freda loses any claim to confidentiality if she makes the information public in some way.

If you are found to have breached confidentiality and caused loss to Freda, the court may order an injunction preventing you from wrongly using her material, or may order you to pay her monetary compensation.

The law of confidentiality can be useful for protecting the interests of the production company. In the process of developing the show, the company along with its employees and consultants may build up valuable know-how about how best to produce and market the show. Information may be obtained about audience figures that are privy to the company, which could be quite valuable. An obligation of confidentiality may apply to the employees and consultants, so that they could be sued if they wrongly use the information. It might also be useful to require key players in the company to enter into confidentiality agreements that include a requirement that if the player leaves the company, they not compete against the company with the same or similar project for an agreed period of time. The non-competition clause in a contract should not be too wide in its scope; otherwise, a court may strike it down for breaching competition laws.

The basic idea behind the law regarding confidentiality is that someone who receives information in confidence should not gain an unfair advantage by having access to the information, and nor should they be entitled to profit from the wrongful use or publication of the information. The information can be given verbally or in writing, or both. The information remains confidential unless and until the information provider allows the information to become public knowledge. If, for example, Freda pitches confidential information about her proposal for *Player Challenge* and then issues a press release outlining the proposal, then the publicly revealed information loses its confidentiality.

So, the person receiving the information in confidence must not use the information in a way that prejudices the interests of the person giving the information. The obligation to deal with the information appropriately applies to the original receiver of the information and anyone else who receives the information and is aware that the information was originally given in confidence. So if Freda pitches her project to you in confidence and you then communicate it to others in your organization and they are aware that you received it in confidence, then they may be successfully sued for breach of confidence if they misuse the information.

One of the advantages of the law regarding confidentiality is that it applies even if the information given does not have copyright. If Freda, for example, only gives verbal information about her project at the pitch meeting, that information will not have copyright, but the law regarding confidentiality may protect it. Even if the information is given in writing, but amounts to a collection of genre ideas or a very broad and general outline of the format structure and therefore does not have copyright, it may nevertheless be protected because it is confidential information. That said, the confidential information must be sufficiently developed and have some attractiveness for a television programme. This does not necessarily mean that there needs to be a full synopsis of the programme; it will very much depend on the circumstances. The nature of the idea may in some cases require extensive development to have any real potential as a format proposal; in other cases the idea may be so powerful that it has sufficient value as a short unelaborated statement of the idea. The essential test is whether the idea is such that it is apparent to an industry player that the concept can be carried into effect. That is it has some attractiveness as a television programme and is something that is capable of being realized as an actuality.

If a pitcher of a project sues for breach of confidence, he or she must establish that; (1) the information was of a confidential nature; (2) the information was communicated in circumstances importing an obligation of confidence; and (3) there has been an unauthorized use of the information to the detriment of the person who originally disclosed the information (i.e. the person pitching the project). The first requirement will be judged against the usage and practices of the industry. For the second requirement there must be an express or implied, obligation to keep the material confidential. Marking the documents 'confidential' or 'in confidence' on each page helps establish that the pitcher intends that the information provided be kept confidential. The test is to ask whether a reasonable person standing in the shoes of the recipient of the information would have realized that upon reasonable grounds the information was being given to him or her in confidence. Finally, the pitcher must prove that the unauthorized use of the information caused them detriment. The detriment may have caused actual or potential loss of earnings.

Licensing the show for broadcast

Once a producer, or more commonly a production company, has acquired all the rights to a show, including purchasing the copyright from the creator if there is one, they can proceed with producing the show. On completion the production company might then license the rights to broadcast the show to a broadcaster. Generally, the rights include licensing the broadcaster to use the copyright material and any other legal rights tied up in the show for broadcast. A license is in effect a grant of permission.

As an example of how licensing legal rights operates; if I provide a licence for someone to enter my land, I am providing him or her permission to enter. I can attach conditions to the licence. For example, I may require the payment of a fee, or only allow the person to enter for a set period of time, or I could allow them in if they mow the lawn, and so on. A significant advantage of a license is that I can retain my underlying rights; that is, my ownership and occupation of the land. More or less the same applies for the producer of a film or TV show. If they own the copyright to the film or TV show, they can license (permit) a broadcaster to broadcast the show, whilst retaining ownership the copyright.

The broadcaster will want to be satisfied that the production company has all the necessary rights tied up in the show before it pays for the licence to broadcast the show (this is not to be confused with a license provided by the government to be able to broadcast; in that case the government is granting a permission to broadcast on certain conditions set out in the broadcast licence). The production company cannot give more than what it's got. So the production company must ensure that all rights are assigned to it before it proceeds to on-license those rights. As an example, a number of parties will have copyright in various components of the show, which need to be assigned to the production company:

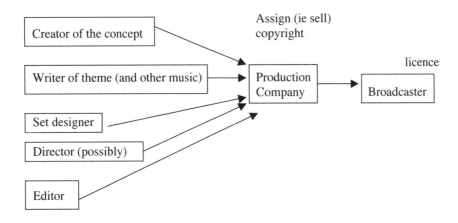

Fig. 9.2 - The assignment and licensing of copyright

The broadcaster's lawyers will check the assignment of copyright contracts held by the production company to ensure there is an unbroken 'chain of title' between the original copyright holders and the production company enabling it to license those rights to the broadcaster. There must be an unbroken chain starting at the creation of an intellectual property right, through to the end use of that right. The term 'intellectual property right' broadly describes knowledge-based rights, including copyright, patents, designs and trademarks.

Freda's other rights

1. *Breach of contract*

Aside from claiming an infringement of copyright and breach of confidentiality, Freda could claim a breach of contract. Circumstances permitting, she could claim breach of an express agreement or of an implied agreement to be paid for the format ideas. An implied contract might exist if in the circumstances in which Freda pitches a project it is well understood in the industry that if a party pitches a project and it is taken up and used in some way, the pitcher is expected to be paid. It helps (but it is not essential) if Freda is an established industry player and that the person to whom she pitches the project is a commissioning editor. It is understood in the industry that where an established scriptwriter or format creator pitches a project to a commissioning editor, for example, that the creator is not offering her proposal for free; she expects to be paid if it leads to the development of a broadcast programme.

One advantage in suing for breach of contract is that there is no necessary requirement for there to be copyright in the ideas pitched (unless the parties agreed otherwise). So the fact that the ideas pitched are not in writing, or the crucial elements are not in writing or some other tangible form, does not itself defeat a claim that a contract was breached. But proving the existence of a contract can be a stumbling block. If there was simply a verbal discussion, it can come down to one party's word against another's. Even if it can be established that there was an agreement (i.e. contract), there can be problems proving precisely what the terms of that agreement were. It is therefore advisable to keep notes of any meetings, which set out the day and time of the meeting, who was present, where the meeting was held and a reasonably concise but comprehensive dot point account of who said what on any salient matters. The notes do not have to be taken during the meeting. If not, they should be written down soon after, when the events of the meeting are still fresh in your mind. You should note down the day and time that you wrote down your notes.

The disadvantage of breach of contract is that the contract only binds the parties to the contract. You can only sue the other party to the contract for an alleged breach. For an alleged copyright infringement, on the other hand, you can successfully sue complete strangers; that is, anyone who allegedly infringed your copyright.

2. *Unjust enrichment*

If there is no contract, it is possible to sue the alleged copycat for unjust enrichment. If there is no contract and no copyright infringement, but a producer takes a creator's proposal and without permission turns it into a programme, then it is possible that the creator could successfully sue the producer for unjust enrichment. To win the case, the creator must establish that the producer was enriched (e.g. made some money) as a result of using the creator's proposal, that the producer was enriched at the creator's expense and that the producer did all this in circumstances which a court would judge to be unjust. This could be established by showing that in all the circumstances of the particular case the producer acted in an unfair way, by effectively 'stealing' the creator's ideas and making a profit from doing so.

Competition law

Unfair competition involves dishonest or fraudulent rivalry in business. It includes imitating the name or appearance of a competitor's products to give the public the impression that the imitator's business is part of the competitor's business, or has the competitor's backing or approval. This activity is known in a number of countries such as the United States, United Kingdom, Australia and New Zealand, as 'passing off'. That is, it involves for example passing off your format as having a competitor's imprimatur. It involves gaining a free ride from the time and expense a competitor put into developing its brand recognition and good reputation in a market.

As a simple example of passing off; if production company A produces a movie called *Friday Night Murder* and production company B produces *Friday Night Murder II* without any consent from production company A, then this may well cause the public to believe that *Murder II* is a sequel to the original. Company B would be gaining an unfair free ride off the back of the time, effort and expense put into the original production by company A. There is also a fair trade argument that the public had developed a confidence in the quality and excitement of the original movie, and therefore was being misled by the copycat into believing that the original producers and creators were involved in the creation of the apparent sequel. The copycat could also be undermining the good reputation and goodwill of company A, denying it the reasonable prospect of successfully producing its own sequel.

'Passing off' has a different name in other jurisdictions. In Germany the owners of a format can sue an alleged copycat if their format is a 'direct appropriation of achievement' - that is, if the copycat show is appropriating the brand recognition and achievements of the original format. The original format owners must prove that the alleged copycat has taken a free ride on the back of the original format owner's achievements. To succeed in this action, the owners of the original format must prove that their format has in fact developed sufficient recognition in the marketplace, that is to say that the format has a 'competitive individual character'. This requires that the original format have sufficiently unique qualities of originality and quality.

The French equivalent to passing off is the action for *confusion dans l'esprit public* and the *agissements parasitaires*. The first involves claiming that the alleged copycat made an extensive or exact imitation of the original format to such a degree that it causes the public to confuse one format with another. The 'public' must be the same public, that is to say, the product or format must appeal to essentially the same audience. To take a non-format example, McDonald's Restaurants probably would not be confused with McDonald's Furnishings as they are aimed at different audiences - or 'publics'. In the case of formats, it might be successfully argued that no confusion would be created if a documentary were made about the social impact of *Big Brother*, as it appeals to a different audience than that which is interested in watching the reality show itself. To be on the safe side, it is possible for the documentary maker to make it clear to the audience that it is not associated with the producers of *Big Brother* by stating that it is an 'unauthorized' account of the making and social impact of *Big Brother*. Even so, the unauthorized use of the *Big Brother* trademark can cause problems.

For an allegation of *agissements parasitaires* it needs to be proved that the alleged copycat parasitically imitated the original format and thereby unfairly benefited from the time and resources and know-how of the original format. This action could well succeed if the copycat imitated the sequences and progressions and used the same show host of the original.

Passing off, like the French action in confusion *dans l'esprit public*, only occurs where confusion is created in the public mind about competing products. In the case of *Green* v. *Broadcasting Corporation of New Zealand* (1989), which we deal with in more detail in the next chapter, it was claimed that the Broadcasting Corporation of New Zealand had passed off its version of *Opportunity Knocks* with that of the original version created in the United Kingdom by Hughie Green. Mr Green failed in his passing off claim because the court said that Mr Green and his show *Opportunity Knocks* had no established reputation in New Zealand, and therefore the New Zealand audience was unlikely to confuse his UK show with the New Zealand show. The general assumption that is often made is that an action in passing off will not succeed if a format is copied in another country in which a producer does not have an established reputation. A recent Australian case suggests that this is not necessarily a correct assumption. The judge in *ConAgra Inc.* v. *McCain Foods (Aust) Pty Limited* (1992:234) said that:

> *The reality of modern international business is that contemporary consumers are not usually concerned about the actual location of the premises of a company or the site of its warehouse or manufacturing plant where the goods are produced, but they are concerned with maintenance of a high level of quality represented by internationally known and famous goods.*

In other words, the world is now much more globalized. Cable and satellite television, and the increasing broadband capacities of the Internet are creating markets that are less defined by national boundaries that they once were. In addition, the market for formats is not limited to TV audiences, there is also a substantial 'wholesale' market where formats are traded; including MIP at Cannes, which we have discussed earlier in this book. Reputation damage and damage to potential sales of formats can be done if a copycat produces an imitating format for another overseas market.

Other grounds for suing an alleged copycat

The alleged copycat is also at risk of being sued on a number of other grounds, depending on the particular circumstances of the alleged copycatting. We will not detail them here. Suffice to say, you could ask your lawyer for advice on the possibilities of success if you sued on these grounds. These grounds include suing for breach of fiduciary duty or constructive trust, negligent misrepresentation, conversion and duress.

If the defendant gained access to information about your project in circumstances in which you entrusted the them to manage the project on your behalf, there may be a fiduciary duty or a constructive trust created, which means that the defendant has to act in your best interests, cannot create a conflict of interest or gain a secret profit from the project. If you have been wrongly advised about the management and development of the project, you might be able to sue for negligent misrepresentation.

If you have required that the defendant hold the project information on your behalf, or they have access to the information, but then use it as if it were their own, then they may be sued for conversion - i.e. for wrongly converting the material to their own use, as if they owned it. They might also be sued for fraud or duress if they tricked you or placed undue pressure on you to relinquishing your rights.

Ancillary rights

Format production companies are increasingly building a wall of rights to protect their investment in new formats. The rights include registering a trademark over the title to the show, creating original theme music and other musical and other sound motifs during the show that help provide it with a unique look and feel (and which have copyright), and registering the design over aspects of the set. One disadvantage of designs and trademarks is that they ultimately need to be registered in each country in which you seek protection. This can be time consuming and expensive. The advantage of copyright is that once you gain copyright in the country in which the work is created, it automatically gains recognition in most countries throughout the world without any need for registration.

Any new inventions created for a TV show, for example a special camera lens or lighting system, might be capable of being patented. The invention will only be able to gain a patent if it is novel, not obvious and is useful, in the sense that it is capable of an industrial application. The invention must be different from what is already publicly known, even if the difference is slight. It must be non-obvious in the sense that it involves an inventive step resulting in something that is new, unexpected, or produces far superior results than is produced by existing products. The invention must also have a useful effect or purpose. A patent lasts for twenty years after registration with the Patents Office. The patent only applies in the country or countries in which a patent is registered.

In some countries, including the United States, it is possible to gain design patents to protect the appearance of an article if the design invention is a new, original and ornamental design for an article of manufacture. The United States and European countries also allow patenting of 'business methods' inventions. These are inventions concerning the buying and selling of items, marketing techniques, financial schemes and strategies for use with sports and games. There may well be under-utilized opportunities to patent business methods arising from games, strategies and schemes used in TV formats.

A production company can also grant a license to the manufacturers of various consumer items, allowing them to print any trademarked item, character or slogan on the items (i.e. merchandising rights) for a fee. Fees and royalties might be charged for any books, DVDs, CDs or any other products that carry copyright and other intellectual property rights associated with the show. Possibilities exist for some format shows, like *Idol* or *Popstar*, for related sound recording contracts.

In summary, there are a wide range of legal rights that can be deployed to protect the interests of the creators of TV formats and the interests of format producers and production houses. In the next chapter we return to the controversy relating to copyright and TV formats. The copyright issues regarding the protection of formats are somewhat unique to the industry and so deserve further examination.

CHAPTER 10

Can there be copyright in formats?

Justin Malbon

It has been a tough year in the world of TV formats. They are under siege from copy-cats after being protected for years by an almost informal agreement to respect intellectual property. In the United States, rival networks NBC and Fox have been slugging it out in court over NBC's The Contender *and Fox's alleged clone* The Next Great Champ. *ABC has also accused Fox of copying its British import* Wife Swap *as* Trading Spouses.

And last week, Pop Idol *creator Simon Fuller began legal action against producer Simon Cowell and Fremantle over a new series,* The X Factor, *which Fuller claims has 32 identical elements.* (Idato 2004)

The question whether there can be copyright in a format is controversial, and the controversy is not confined to a handful of countries. There are very few (if any) countries in which it can be categorically stated that the law can or cannot protect a format. This raises the question as to what precisely we mean by a 'format', which we will consider next. A decade or two ago it was relatively safe to claim that the law of copyright cannot protect formats. Greater doubt surrounds such a claim today. There have been a number of cases that have laid the basis for a finding in a future case (with the right sort of factual scenario) that copyright exists in a particular format and is infringed by a copycat format.

The reasons for legal doubt appear to arise from the way in which courts have framed the copyright question when dealing with a claim that there has been an infringement of copyright in a format. The courts have adopted one of two general approaches to the question. The first approach analogizes a format programme with a play, or TV drama. Dramas are usually scripted. There is no doubt that there is copyright in an original script, nor is there any doubt that copyright exists in a dramatic performance of the script. Format shows, however, are generally unscripted. There tends to be a broad outline of the events that are to take place, but other than that there is no script and therefore no performance based on a script. Consequently, a court that frames the copyright question this way when deciding whether copyright exists in a format is likely to find that there is no copyright.

The second approach takes the format programme on its own merits. The question asked is whether the completed TV show, or the pitch documents for a TV format, evidence an original format with a discernibly distinct structure. Here the question is: does the format show when taking the show as a whole and its particular way of combining tension points, the rules of the game and so on, develop a sufficiently coherent and recognizable structure? If the answer is in the affirmative, a court is more likely to find there is copyright in the format. If a court does find that there is copyright in a format show, this does not necessarily mean that the show's producer has won any action against an alleged copycat. The court must also find that the alleged copycat has substantially copied the format. This is often not easy to establish. There may be a number of genre elements that are similar, but the overall look and feel of the two shows may be sufficiently dissimilar, resulting in a finding that there is no infringement.

Courts tend to decide whether there is copyright in a format either by considering it as a distinct work or by analogizing it with a scripted play. To understand how these two approaches have developed, we need to gain further insights into the workings of copyright law itself. A few generalizations can be made that more or less apply in most countries. First, the law attempts a high wire act between allowing the free exchange of ideas and creative pursuit on the one hand, and acknowledging and protecting the work of creators and protecting 'industrial' output in the form of broadcasts, films and phonograms (i.e. CDs, DVDs, mp3s etc.) on the other. If we take a self-interested producer, we see similar competing interests. On the one hand, the producer will want to protect her own work from infringement, but on the other hand would not want the copyright in other creative works to be so extensive as to inhibit her from creating new programmes. New creative works will invariably have elements from existing works; there is nothing entirely new under the sun.

The second generalization, which we mentioned in the previous chapter, flows from the first point, which is the law will not protect creative ideas unless they exist in some tangible form. Tangible forms include writing the ideas on paper, typing it into a word processor, recording them on a tape recorder or digital recorder, filming it and so on. The third generalization, which again we mentioned in the previous chapter, is that the tangible work must be original. The law is generous on this point. What we have written does not have to be novel. It can be boring (we hope this isn't!), unremarkable, inelegant and derivative (in the general sense), but it cannot be a literal copy or a substantial copy of a prior work.

The differing approaches in various countries to copyright tend to create uncertainty regarding formats, because they invariably sit in a grey area. The differences of approach arise in some cases from differences in the law and in other cases from differences of approach to the interpretation of the law. German courts tend to be less likely to find copyright than say a Dutch court. British courts could go either way, depending on the facts of the case and the particular judges hearing the matter. The United States is hard to pick for a range of reasons, including the differences of laws and approaches in the various State and Federal jurisdictions.

There have been more cases fought out in courts in which the party claiming copyright to a format has lost than those in which the claimant has won. One of the few successful cases was won by Celador, the producers of *Who Wants to be a Millionaire?* Celador gained an injunction in a Danish court against Denmark Radio prohibiting them from broadcasting a similar show called (when translated) *Double or Quits*. The injunction was not contested and Denmark Radio paid a substantial sum in damages (*Celador Productions Ltd v. Danmarks Radio, 2000*). The fact that there is a distinct minority of successful court actions might suggest that a court is unlikely to find that copyright exists in a format show. That conclusion, in our view, is somewhat simplistic. It is true to say that some cases take a fairly hard line; this approach is particularly evident in Germany and to some extent the United Kingdom. A more generous approach is detectable in cases decided in New Zealand, the Netherlands and the United States. In total, there are not many decided cases throughout the world dealing with TV formats. It would therefore be wrong, in our view, to assume that there is little or no risk of breaching copyright if you directly copy (with or without a few minor changes) other format shows. To explain our position, we will outline the way the law deals with copyright. In order to understand the operation of the two approaches to the copyright question, we need to gain a better understanding of how the law of copyright itself works. After considering what we mean by the term 'format', we will consider the scope of copyright in broad terms; what material is protected by copyright; the way in which a court analogizes formats with dramas; and the way in which a court considers a format as a distinct work.

What is a format?

The law does not recognize a 'format' as a distinct entity entitled in itself to legal protection. Nor is there a generally accepted legal definition of a format. This has not prevented legal commentators from offering suggested definitions. Shelly Lane defines it as 'the fixed structure of a programme which is repeated week after week, giving the programme its character, dramatic movement, identity, and, incidentally, its marketability' (Lane 1992: 26). What is important, she adds, is that while the content will change from week to week, the nature of the type of material will remain the same. Frank Fine, after admitting that there is no settled definition, offers the observation that:

> a format generally is considered to be a written presentation setting out the framework within which the central characters of a proposed program will operate and includes the setting, theme, and premise or general story line of the program. (Fine 1985: 51)

His definition confines itself to the written proposals, and does not mention completed programmes. Arguably, his definition can easily be extended to include the production bible for a completed programme or series. As well as TV shows, formats probably include the storylines and presentation of computer games, and drama and situation comedy series. Indeed, it may also extend to non-fiction 'formats' such as the nightly news, talk shows, and TV magazine formats.

The formats industry

Even taking a relatively narrow definition of a format, it covers an enormous amount of international business. Summarizing from Chapter 7, Endemol, the creators of *Big Brother*, alone creates over 18,000 hours of television and has more than 3,000 employees. It had a turnover of over €850m in 2002. The company has subsidiaries and joint ventures in 21 countries, including the major European markets, the United States, Latin America, South Africa and Australia. The Cologne based RTL (which bought out Pearsons Television, changing its name to Fremantle Media) is heavily involved with format programmes and had a turnover of nearly €5b in the 2003-4 financial year. This is big business in anyone's language.

One may wonder how the multibillion dollar format business can operate if there is no specific or adequate legal protection. Why would a broadcaster bother paying millions of dollars for a product it could simply copy? There are a number of possible reasons for a viable format market. First, the legal protections may not be as weak as they first appear. There are an increasing number of law cases suggesting that there can be copyright in a format, as we will see in our discussion later in this chapter. The courts are increasingly aware of the economic size and value of the industry, and are therefore less likely to be dismissive of its intrinsic value and more likely to view any close copying of a format, which invariably involves considerable time and expense in its development, as a copyright infringement. The changing mood in the courts raises legal uncertainty for potential copycats. Purchasing the rights to a format, on the other hand, buys peace of mind for the production house and the broadcaster. It greatly reduces the risk of the creators of the original format finding out about the copycat during its production and issuing an injunction stopping production - which can make investors and broadcasters extremely nervous and delay production.

Second, purchasing the rights to a format invariably grants the production house the rights to any theme music, graphics and set designs. The production house also gains access to know-how, including the audience figures in a number of territories and the production bible. It may also be able to call on the expertize of the producers of successful productions of the format in other territories. There can often be a number of subtle elements to a successful format that may not be obvious to a copycat who simply relies on viewing tapes of a successful format for designing their version of the programme. These subtle elements can sometimes make all the difference between ratings success and failure.

United Kingdom attempts reform

Although a format programme is not bereft of legal protections, a number of failed attempts were made in the United Kingdom during the 1990s to enhance the legislative protection of formats. An attempt was made to amend the Broadcasting Act to prohibit substantial copying of a format. Of interest is the way in which the proposed legislative amendments defined a format; it was defined as a 'format programme' or a 'format proposal'. A format *proposal* was defined as a plan, recorded in a material form, for a format programme. A format *programme* was defined as being a broadcast or cable programme that is intended or suitable to be one of a series and as having elements of variability or unpredictability as well as established format features. A non-exclusive set of examples of the features of a series for it to qualify as a format was set out in the draft legislation. To qualify as a format under the draft legislation, the features when taken together must:

• amount to an original format;

• be intended or suitable to be common to most of the broadcasts in a series; and

- be intended or suitable to be peculiar to the series to enable the audience to distinguish that series from others.

The required feature, that the series be original, repeats an existing requirement under the copyright law, which provides that copyright only applies to original works; as we will see in our discussion below. The third feature, that the audience must be able to distinguish the series from other existing series, effectively restates the test applied in a number of format cases decided by the courts. In those cases the courts have said that they apply both an objective test (or extrinsic test) and a subjective test (or intrinsic test). The objective/extrinsic test involves identifying the various elements that comprise a format and comparing each of them with the elements in an alleged copycat format to see if there are similarities. The subjective/intrinsic tests involves comparing the two formats as a whole from the perspective of an ordinary member of the audience and deciding whether he or she would consider one programme format to be a substantial copy of the other.

The second feature in the UK legislative proposal, that the format be intended or suitable to be common to most of the broadcasts in a series, is probably stating the obvious. That is, a format is never a one-off programme, like a feature film or one-off TV drama.

So the three features set out under proposed amendment to the UK legislation arguably restate requirements under the existing law. That said, it favours one legal approach to deciding format disputes over another. The proposed amendment sought to mandate an approach by which the courts consider a format as a distinct work as opposed to analogizing it with a scripted play, feature film or TV drama. The amendment was a reaction to the controversial case of *Green* v. *Broadcasting Corporation of New Zealand* (1989), which effectively analogized a format with a play.

Hughie Green was the author, producer and host of a popular UK talent quest show during the 1960s and 1970s called *Opportunity Knocks*. He brought a legal action against the Broadcasting Corporation of New Zealand for its 1978 series called (believe it or not) *Opportunity Knocks*. The lawyers for the New Zealand broadcasters conceded that the New Zealand broadcaster copied all the essential elements of the UK series, without permission from Mr Green. Indeed, Mr Green found out about the New Zealand series by mere chance.

Mr Green wrote fairly rudimentary outlines for the series and for each episode. They set out stock phrases including: 'For [name of person] opportunity knocks'; and 'This is your show, folks, and I do mean you', (it appears that NZBC took that phrase rather literally!); and 'It's make your mind up time'. Each contestant was introduced by his or her own sponsor and the scripts for each episode set out rather broadly the points on which contestants would be interviewed. The winner of each episode was decided by the results of viewer postal votes and the results shown on a 'clapometer', which measured the volume of the studio audiences' applause for each performance. The New Zealanders copied all these elements, yet the Privy Council, which was the final court of appeal, found that there was no infringement of copyright.

How did the court arrive at this rather surprising result? Essentially, the trial judge who heard the case in New Zealand ruled that the Hughie Green's 'scripts' for the series and for each episode were rudimentary and therefore did little more than express general ideas, which did not gain copyright. The law does not protect commonplace ideas, or genres, as we saw in the last chapter in which we used the example of *Punch-Drunk Love*. The law does not provide copyright protection to the general concept of a game show, a quiz show, a reality show or a quest show. Just as there is no copyright in the general concept of a boy meets girl story, or a romance, a thriller or a comedy. Copyright will exist in a work at a certain point of specificity. A movie script, for example, might be a romance, but in the telling will have specific characters who interact in a way that conforms to a relatively unique plot. At a certain (hard to define) point of specificity the script will be more detailed than a mere boy meets girl scenario and amount to being a distinct story in its own right. Anyone who substantially copies that story will infringe the copyright of the author in the original script.

The trial judge in Green dealt with the question of whether there was copyright in *Opportunity Knocks* by effectively treating the question the same way as he would decide whether there was copyright in a play, TV drama or feature film. That is, he first looked for a script and asked himself whether the script upon which the 'play' was performed was sufficiently original to gain copyright. To understand why he adopted this approach it is necessary to pause a moment to gain a sense of how the law is framed for dealing with copyright issues.

In a number of countries, including the United Kingdom, New Zealand, Australia, Canada and the United States, copyright can be gained in literary, dramatic, artistic and musical works. So, the law does not directly ask the question; is there copyright in a particular show. Rather the question is whether a particular claimed work is an original literary, dramatic, artistic or musical work, which might happen to be related to a particular show. The work might be a script, production bible, dramatic work, musical score or set design. Each of these works will have copyright, not the format show itself.

This all seems a little confusing. We can attempt to clarify this point by taking the relatively straightforward example of a TV drama. In the diagram on the next page, we can see the relevant elements (for copyright purposes) that go into creating the TV drama, which we will call *Law and Disorder*.

Many of us would intuitively consider that the question is whether or not copyright exists in the TV show *Law and Disorder* itself. But the law does not quite see things that way. It asks whether a literary, dramatic, artistic or music work exists; which is a different way of framing the question as to whether there is copyright in the TV show. What then is a literary, dramatic, artistic or musical work?

A *literary work* is any work other than a dramatic or musical work that is written, spoken (but exists in some tangible form, for example on tape or digitally recorded) or sung (but again exists in some tangible form). A literary work includes scripts, treatments, outlines, and song lyrics. Almost anything committed to writing, whether on paper, typed into a computer or other tangible form will gain copyright the instant it takes tangible form, so long as it is an 'original' work. The performance of a literary work also has copyright. That is, the unauthorized

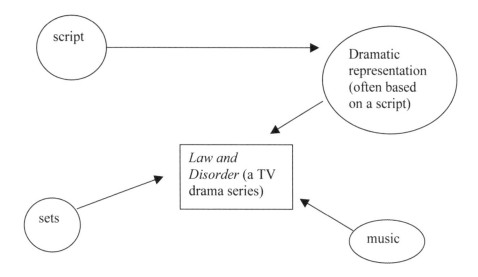

Figure 10.1 Elements of a TV drama under copyright

performance of a script or a play will breach the scriptwriter's or playwright's copyright. In some countries, for example Canada, the script itself is considered to be a dramatic work.

A *dramatic work*, must be (1) a work of action; and (2) capable of being performed. The requirement of 'being performed' is interpreted very liberally, and includes a performance seen on film, even if that performance is physically impossible to perform (*Norowzian* v. *Arks Ltd.* (No. 2) (2000)). It includes, for example, an actor's performance edited by 'jump cuts' or rendered through computer imaging. Even cartoon performances by Daffy Duck can be a dramatic work. A dramatic work also includes mime and dance.

A *musical work* is any work of music, but does not include the lyrics - which are a literary work. So a song may have the copyright in the music held by the person who wrote the music, and the copyright in the lyrics held by the person who wrote the lyrics. It is possible, of course, that this will be one and the same person.

An *artistic work* includes any graphic work, including a painting, diagram, map, drawing, plan, chart, a photograph (but not a film) and a sculpture and a collage. An architectural work can also be an artistic work, being any fixed structure, building or model of the building or structure. A set for the TV show could be an artistic work. Also, any artistic craftsmanship would be capable of copyright protection.

A *database and compilation* can also have copyright. A number of countries have introduced laws providing for copyright to databases. The UK Copyright and Rights in Databases Regulations 1997 (SI 1997/3032), for example, has created database rights in the United Kingdom. In addition, the UK *Copyright, Designs and Patents Act* 1988 has also made it explicit that copyright applies to compilations. A database is defined as a collection of independent works, data or other materials which: (a) are arranged in a systematic or methodical way; and (b) are individually accessible by electronic or other means. The author of a database of questions for a quiz show could hold copyright in the database. Gough suggests the possibility of a format show itself being a database in the sense that it is a collection of independent works (i.e. the script, diagrams for the sets and the musical score) that are arranged in a systematic or methodical way and are accessible by electronic means (i.e. via the TV set or in some cases the Internet) (Gough 2002: 28). This might be stretching the meaning of 'database' somewhat, and it is probably unnecessary to do so in any event. A court can use more conventional copyright law approaches to find the existence of copyright.

Under the German Copyright Act, copyright can be gained for the creators of literary, scientific, and artistic works. A work capable of gaining copyright can only be 'personal intellectual creations', that is to say something that is an expression of the creator's individuality. And so questions can arise as to the 'degree of creation', 'degree of achievement' or 'degree of composition' employed by the creator. It is possible under German law to gain copyright in an oral expression of a thought, providing it has a sufficient degree of personal intellectual creation.

In France, copyright applies to the 'intellectual work' (*oeuvre de l'esprit*). Again, originality is required, that is to say, there needs to be an expression of the creator's personality (*empreinte de la personnalité de l'auteur*). Protection applies to a number of categories of works, including audiovisual works, which is to say a 'series of moving pictures'. The claimant must prove that their work is more than a mere idea, and has become a detailed, elaborated and original format.

A TV show, including a format show, is usually comprised of a number of copyright works, including the script (if there is one), production bibles and other production documents, the music, any database of compiled questions and the set design. There is no copyright in the show itself, but in the various copyright works that together constitute the show.

The *Green Case* on appeal

Mr Green lost his trial against the Broadcasting Corporation of New Zealand, and so appealed the decision to the New Zealand Court of Appeal. Of the three judges who heard the appeal, one found in his favour and the other two against. One of the judges, Justice Somers, agreed with the trial judge, saying that *Opportunity Knocks* was not a dramatic work because there was insufficient certainty in the 'script'. In other words, the judge was tied to old assumptions that a dramatic performance, like a play, must necessarily be based on a script. The other two judges disagreed with this reasoning. They both said that copyright was not limited to written material, and that there could be copyright in other tangible forms such as film or videotape. As the UK *Opportunity Knocks* series was recorded on tape, it existed in a tangible form, and therefore met one of the necessary criteria for copyright. But one of the two judges thought that despite that, the show was merely a 'basic concept underlying a series of changing dramatic works', and therefore incapable of gaining copyright (*Green* 1989: 15). In other words, he thought that the series was simply a collection of commonplace ideas or genres without any discernable original structure.

The minority judge who found in favour of Mr Green had the better view in our opinion. He said the essential question was 'whether or not an idea developed into an original continuing or repeated dramatic format, could be the subject of copyright protection' (*Green* 1989: 20). He added that copyright could exist in the show if it has a recognizable framework or structure that imposes a shape upon the other constituent parts of the show. In the end, he said, it is a question of degree as to whether there is a sufficient perceived structure in the series of shows (*Green* 1989: 20). So the question, as far as the minority judge was concerned, was whether there was an overall format, framework or structure evident in the series, which repeats in each episode.

What we find in the reasoning of the three Court of Appeal judges is a contest between two approaches to considering copyright. One approach involves analogizing a format with a play. The question the court asks is: where's the script, and is the script an original work? The second approach involves asking whether there is a sufficiently recognizable and original framework or structure in the series. If so, copyright exists in the series format.

Hughie Green lost in the New Zealand Court of Appeal, and so further appealed the case to the Privy Council in London. The Privy Council dealt with the matter in a cursory way. In a two-page judgment, they found it difficult to work out what it was in the nature of the work that gained copyright protection: was it the repetition, the structure or the package, the judges asked themselves? They claimed difficulty in distilling out what precisely in *Opportunity Knocks* was the 'work' (as defined by the Copyright Act) that is entitled to copyright protection. The judges noted that there were a number of distinctive features of the series that could be identified, but they professed difficulty in finding sufficient unity in the performances of each episode to amount to an 'original dramatic work' (*Green* 1989: 20). They also had difficulty isolating the allegedly distinctive features that existed throughout the series (i.e. the original dramatic work) from the changing material that appeared in each episode.

The court did not commit to either the analogy with a play or the sufficiently recognizable structure approach. It appeared to say that *Opportunity Knocks* did not move beyond being a collection of commonplace elements, which lacked any distinct structure. If so, this seems an extraordinary conclusion. It suggests that *Opportunity Knocks* is undifferentiated from any other talent quest. Although some critics may claim that all talent shows, or all quiz shows are all much the same, the law (as we have seen) does not require novelty or a high degree of originality for a work to gain copyright. Some critics have suggested that the Privy Council in *Green* put their aesthetic values about what qualifies as good television ahead of a dispassionate application of the law.

A British court back in 1911 cautioned that a judge is not entitled to take a personal view when considering copyright issues about whether he believes a work is worthy or appropriate for audiences. In the case of *Perkin* v. *Ray Bros* (1911), the court was required to consider whether there can be copyright in a vaudeville show, which is a collection of skits. The court issued a stop order (an injunction) preventing another producer from substantially copying a vaudeville show despite it attracting audiences 'of a certain class'. The court granted the injunction despite the fact that in the court's view there was no connected dramatic interest; that it was simply scenes loosely hung together; the script was an outline and the personality of the comedian largely went to construct it.

On this basis, there is no fundamental reason why a heavy use of genre elements, minimal scripting and lack of literary quality in itself disqualifies a format show from copyright protection.

Survivor versus Big Brother

An example of the application of the recognizable structure approach to considering whether a TV format has copyright can be found in the case of *Castaway Television Productions Ltd* v. *Endemol Entertainment International*, which was decided by a Netherlands court on 27 June 2002. The UK company, Castaway Television Productions, the creators of *Survivor*, sued Endemol, the creators of *Big Brother*, for breach of copyright, amongst other things. Castaway claimed that *Big Brother* was a substantial copy of their *Survivor* format. In deciding the matter, the court first had to ask whether there was any copyright in the *Survivor* format, and second, whether *Big Brother* infringed that copyright. The court found that there was copyright in the *Survivor* format, but that *Big Brother* did not infringe the copyright.

In deciding whether there was copyright in the *Survivor* format, the court considered whether copyright existed in the written programme proposals. The proposal had three parts: (1) seventeen pages outlining the format, with biographies of its creators; (2) ten pages setting out the rules of the game; and (3) fifteen pages setting out the production strategy. The court asked whether the material was sufficiently original and sufficiently detailed. Castaway Productions argued that there were twelve elements to the proposal, and although each single element itself was not original, the way in which the elements were combined created an original work. The claimed elements of the *Survivor* format were:

1. A small group of very different people are separated from the outside world and are thus severely restricted in their freedom of movement;

2. The group is being followed by TV cameras and one or more presenters;

3. The group is being filmed 24 hours a day;

4. The programme is set up as a daily record in which the reporting period is always one day;

5. The group has to fulfil tasks set by the producers and earn bonuses;

6. The group must be self supporting;

7. The group themselves vote who to remove or who to nominate for removal; the participants must constantly choose between their own interests and their loyalty towards the group;

8. The group is selected by psychologists and the producer;

9. The group is not allowed to have contact with the outside world unless allowed by the producers;

10. The group may only take a limited number of personal items with them;

11. The members of the group are asked to maintain a personal video diary to record their impression of the experiment; and

12. The last remaining participant wins the big prize, the rest get nothing.

The court agreed that there was copyright in the format. In other words, it did not matter that each element alone had no copyright; it is the way in which those elements are combined that can create a unique work. There is no magic number of elements that must exist before an original work is created; it will very much depend on the particular circumstances of each case. As we mentioned in the previous chapter, a test was provided by US Supreme Court Judge Leaned Hand for deciding the point at which a rather abstract descriptions of a play build to a level of specificity to become identifiable as a copyright work. Judge Leaned Hand's 'abstractions test' tends to be more of a description of a general process of reasoning to be used by a court than a relatively precise way of determining the dividing line between copyright and non-copyright.

Chafee, a US legal commentator, offers another test, which he calls the 'pattern' test. Under this test, copyright exists where the work reveals a pattern, which is to say there is a sequence of events and interplay between the characters (Chafee 1945: 513-4). So a story that is a romance in which boy meets girl lacks a pattern. There is no sequence of events, other than the very general idea that a boy meets a girl, nor is there any interplay between the characters. But as the story becomes more elaborated, with a sequence of events leading to the first meeting, the initial interest by the boy and disinterest, maybe even disgust, from the girl, and then other sequences of events taking place and interplay occurring between the characters leading to them both falling in love. At some point, we have something more than genre and the commonplace, instead we have a distinct pattern to the story. Although this test is somewhat useful, there is room for different conclusions about where to draw the line in any particular case. Fine proposes a hybrid of the abstractions and the patterns test and comes up with what he describes as his 'expression' test (Fine 67). This, he says, requires us to test the comprehensiveness of the depth and breadth of the work. Thus, the essence of infringement is not in copying a general theme, but in the work's particular expression through similarities of treatment, details, scenes, events and characterizations (see *Reyher* v. *Children's Television* Workshop (1976:91)).

Fine claims support for this approach by the court in *Nintendo of America Inc.* v. *Elcon Industries Inc.* (1982), where it was prepared to protect video games like *Donkey Kong*. The court emphasized that copyright applied to the combination of elements that comprise the video game, and not just its fixed sequences. The court in *Nintendo* said that the 'expression' of ideas which gain copyright protection include the 'characters, obstacles and background as well as the sequence of play of the game'. In another case the court said that the author's copyright over a number of games included the 'audiovisual expression of various game ideas [including] the distinctive colour and design of the space ships and other players, as well as the sound accompanying the playing of the games'. That is, copyright protects the game as a whole, including the theme of the game, the interaction of characters or obstacles, the development of the game story and even the setting (mazes or outer space). Fine argues that the protection given to the video game formats logically and necessarily extends to TV formats (Fine 1985: 65).

The next question the court considered in the Netherlands case of *Castaway* v. *Endemol* was whether Endemol had infringed Castaway Production's *Survivor* format. The court concluded that there was no copyright infringement. So, merely proving you have copyright in a format does not necessarily mean that another format, which you believe is similar to yours, infringes your copyright. Establishing copyright is only a first step. We will return to the *Castaway Productions* case later in this chapter in the next part dealing with infringement.

Infringement

Assuming that there is copyright in a format show, the next question is whether an alleged copycat has infringed your copyright. An infringement of copyright occurs where there is a copying of a 'substantial part' of another copyright work. In a number of common law countries, the quality of the work copied is relevant in deciding whether there is an infringement of literary and dramatic works.

So the mere copying of another copyright work is not in itself an infringement. If we quote a sentence in this book from another copyright work, there will not necessarily be an infringement. There are two possible reasons it is not an infringement; the first is because the copied material was not a substantial copy of the copyright work, and second, in some countries, including the United States, a fair use defence exists. That is, even if there is a substantial copying, there might be a fair use of the copied material.

The test for substantial copying is a qualitative rather than a quantitative test. Generally, there is no fixed 5 per cent or 10 per cent rule that allows copying of a specified proportion of a work. A practice appears to have developed with some publishers that require that their authors copy no more than a fixed percentage of other copyright works in their books; and in some cases there are arrangements with collection organizations (which collect royalties on behalf of their clients) and institutions such as universities where only a defined proportion of material can be copied. In most cases these are either contractual arrangements or industry practices that have developed, which are not required by the copyright law.

Under copyright law it is quality that counts. That is not to say that quantity is irrelevant. Obviously, copying a substantial quantity of a work, even if it involves copying low quality aspects of a work, could itself constitute substantial copying and therefore an infringement. The point is copyright law is not fixated upon formulaic percentages for deciding whether there is an infringement. It looks to the substance of the copying. Copying a three minute sequence of a fairly commonplace street scene setting from a two-hour film, for example, might not be an infringement, whilst a twenty-second cleverly and originally composed combat scene from the same film might be an infringement. A similar example can be used in the case of music; copying a two-minute fairly commonplace blues riff might not be an infringement, and yet a thirty-second copy of a highly original segment may be an infringement.

The test is whether the part copied is a substantial, vital, and essential part of the copied work, or is of dramatic value and importance. Having said that, we admit the law is not entirely consistent in its approach to deciding copyright infringement, just as it is not consistent in deciding what material gains copyright and what does not. We will refer to a few cases in some detail to give a sense of the way in which courts have dealt with infringement regarding television programmes.

In the US case of *Chuck Blore and Don Richman Inc.* v. *20/20 Advertising* (1987) the claimant advertising company sued the defendant eyewear company and its advertising agency for the alleged copyright infringement of their advertisement. Both the claimant's and the defendant's advertisements used the same celebrity, Deborah Shelton from *Dallas*, and the same rapid-edit montage style of twenty close-up and medium shots against a green background. They showed close-ups of Ms Shelton trying to fix her hair, long shots of her wearing different clothes and hairstyles, and medium shots of her wearing different clothes and hairstyles. The products advertised and the words spoken by Ms Shelton were completely different, so there was no allegation of copying of the textual elements. When the defendant set the advertising brief for their client they said that they would produce an advert similar to *Chuck Blore's* (the claimant's), which (they added in the brief) 'were excellent'.

In deciding whether there was an infringement of the claimant's copyright, the judge said that the test here was whether there is a substantial similarity between the copyright elements of the two works (*Chuck Blore* (1987) at 679). He added that the question is what elements have copyright. Can the rapid style editing, and the way the advert was composed, have copyright? The judge said that 'Whether characterized as an advertising gimmick or "Maddison Avenue" kitsch, the choice of a particular editing style is nonetheless an expressive artistic element for the purposes of copyright law' (*Chuck Blore* (1987) at Fn 5). He added that, by analogy, copyright protection for photographs extends to the choice of subject matter and 'such features as the photographer's selection of lighting, shading, positioning and timing', and so could also apply to the artistic choices in the way that a moving picture is created (*Chuck Blore* (1987) at 677). He also noted that Circular R45 of the US Copyright Office stated copyright existed in concepts behind motion pictures that are embodied in a number of different concrete forms of creative expression such as dialogue, dramatic action, camera work, visual effects, editing, music and so forth (*Chuck Blore* (1987) at 677). So the artistic expression reflecting the unique perspective of individual creators is protected, but not archetypical similarities in plot, setting and character development (*Chuck Blore* (1987) at 678).

The test applied by the judge for deciding whether there was infringement was first to assess the similarities of ideas between the two advertisements by comparing objective similarities in the details of the works. This he described as an extrinsic analysis, and he allowed expert testimony to assist the court. Second, if there are substantial similarities in ideas, the judge must decide whether an ordinary reasonable person viewing the two adverts would think that one was a substantial copy of the other. This involves an intrinsic analysis. Here the judge does not rely on expert testimony, only on his or her own assessment of how the reasonable person would assess them. The question is whether the ordinary observer would regard the aesthetic appeal of the two adverts as the same. That is whether the total concept and feel of the two series of commercials are substantially similar. Thus, he said, it is the presence of substantial similarities rather than differences that determines whether infringement exists. 'That is the "existence of differences will not negate infringement unless they so outweigh similarities that the similarities can only be deemed inconsequential within the total context of" the work' (*Chuck Blore* (1987) at 679).

In this case, the judge found that the defendant did infringe the claimant's copyright in the original advertisement. 'The ordinary reasonable person', he said, 'would simply fail to perceive the differences between the two adverts and would conclude that the aesthetic appeal of the commercials is the same' (*Chuck Blore* (1987) at 681).

Contrast this factual finding with the UK case of *Norowzian* (1998) where the court considered whether an advertisement for Guinness infringed the copyright in a show-reel called *Joy*. The advertisement showed a full glass of Guinness on a stool in front of camera. Behind the glass a man, in a sequence of jump cuts, moved back and forth, close to and then back from the glass of Guinness. *Joy* also showed a glass of beer in front of the camera and a man moving back and forth in a series of jump cuts. The creator of the show-reel had been invited by Guinness' advertising agency to make an advert based on his show-reel, but he declined the invitation. Another director was brought in and shown the *Joy* show-reel and was obviously influenced by it. The court found that there was copyright in the dramatic performance shown in the show-reel, but that there was no infringement. The court said that the subject-matter of the two films is very different and that the striking similarity between the filming and editing styles and techniques used by the two directors was not enough in itself to constitute an infringement.

An example of the approach used in *Chuck Blore* is found in the Netherlands case of *Castaway* v. *Endemol*, which we mentioned earlier in this chapter. You will recall that the court found that Castaway Productions had copyright in their *Survivor* format. The question the court next had to consider was whether the *Big Brother* format was an infringement of the *Survivor* format. The court approached the question in more or less the same way the court did in *Chuck Blore*, despite the fact that case was not referred to and the fact that court was obviously not applying US law.

We mentioned earlier the twelve elements that the court found together comprised the *Survivor* format. When the court considered whether *Big Brother* infringed the *Survivor* format, it first considered how many of the *Big Brother* elements were substantially the same as the *Survivor* elements. This approach is similar to the extrinsic analysis approach adopted in *Chuck Blore*. The Dutch court found that there were no recognizable similarities between the two formats on most elements, but agreed that there was substantial similarity regarding elements nine to eleven. This was not enough to amount to infringement. As an example, the court compared the common element in both formats in which a small group of people are separated from the outside world. In *Survivor* the group is on an island or remote place, whereas in *Big Brother* they are confided to a house, which may or may not be in a remote place. The common element that the group are followed by TV cameras is also very differently executed by the two formats. In one case the camera crew follow members of the group as they travel over the terrain, make camp or undergo various tasks. In the other, the house is filled with surveillance cameras.

As an added test for judging whether there was an infringement through substantial copying, the Dutch court made an overall subjective judgement of whether the *Survivor* series appeared to be a substantial copy of *Big Brother*. This assessment involves much the same approach as the intrinsic analysis adopted in *Chuck Blore*. The court found that the two programmes were substantially different, and therefore there was no infringement.

A more or less similar approach was adopted by the Munich Higher Court in the *Spot-on* decision (1999). The court found that the creator of a game show had copyright to his 23 page concept document for his proposal for a series called *Augenblix*. The document outlined the aim of the series, the set design, and the rules of the game in which contestants guessed commercials from a brief excerpt. The creator also wrote a script and produced a pilot. In March 1996 he submitted the script, concept document and pilot to a broadcaster, which then declined the proposal. Two years later the broadcaster broadcast a daily show called *Spot-on*, which had many of the characteristics of *Augenblix*. Although the court found that the creator had copyright to *Augenblix,* it also found that *Spot-on* was not a substantial copy of the proposed programme.

The court considered each of the elements common to *Augenblix* and *Spot-on*. The element involving contestants guessing commercials was found to be commonplace and not capable of copyright. The speed-guessing element (like beat the buzzer in a quiz show) was again considered commonplace, along with the memory game element. In *Augenblix* only a brief segment of the commercial was shown in the memory component, whereas the entire commercial was shown in *Spot-on*. The 'music round', in which contestants guessed and assigned jingles to particular commercials was again considered a commonplace idea. So the various elements, when considered separately, were seen to be commonplace and incapable in themselves of gaining copyright. Even when the two shows were considered as a whole and compared with each other the court found that *Spot-on* was substantially different from *Augenblix*. The creator, having won round one (with a finding he had copyright in *Augenblix*), lost round two (with a finding that there was no substantial copying).

It is difficult without seeing the two shows to form our own opinion as to whether the outcome of the *Spot-on* decision was fair or not. The reasoning appears quite reasonable and fair. However, one cannot help get the feeling that the broadcaster had the advantage of its particular position to gain access to ideas and then re-work them to avoid a copyright breach (and no-doubt to improve on the

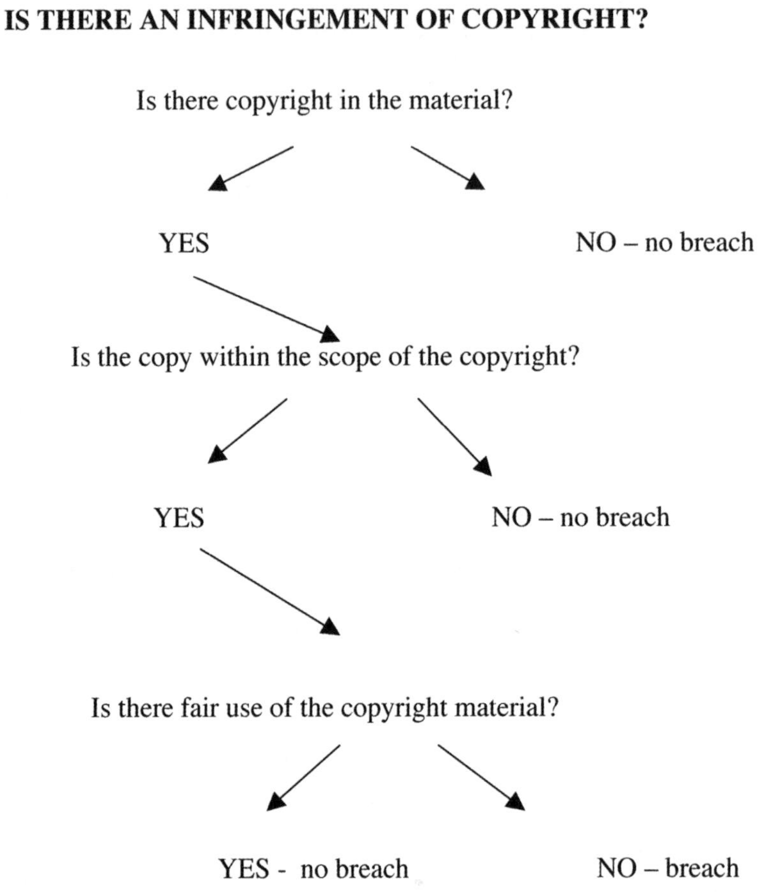

IS THERE AN INFRINGEMENT OF COPYRIGHT?

Is there copyright in the material?

YES   NO – no breach

Is the copy within the scope of the copyright?

YES   NO – no breach

Is there fair use of the copyright material?

YES - no breach   NO – breach

Figure 10.2 Copyright test

initial proposal) in order to present a programme without acknowledging and rewarding the creativity of the effective originator of the programme. The particular vulnerability of the creator who pitches a proposal to a broadcaster or production company is ameliorated to some extent by the law relating to confidentiality and competition law, which we dealt with in the previous chapter.

Finally, even in situations where there is substantial copying, the defence of fair use exists in a number of countries, including the United States. A parody, for example, can be a fair use even if it copies a number of essential elements of the programme it is parodying. To succeed with this defence, it must be shown that the allegedly infringing work adds something new, either by adopting a different purpose than the original work or adopting a different overall character to the original.

CHAPTER 11

Conclusion

This book has been concerned to identify a central component of the current epoch of television. The stage exhibits a distinct break with the recent past. With its reconfiguration of new technologies of delivery, reception and storage, new agencies and players, new contents and new financial arrangements, the medium has changed markedly from what it has been, justifying the name of multi-channel television.

Even before the emergence of a global trade in TV formats, television had already seen one major shift in terms of business arrangements in the arenas of production and distribution. When television was inaugurated in many places over 50 years ago, a familiar system of production obtained.

This was oblivious to the language spoken on and off screen and irrespective of whether the system in question was commercial, public service or state controlled. The system involved television stations conceiving of their function as both producer and broadcast distributor of programmes made in-house. To this end, stations very often had many hundreds of employees filling roles in such areas as the artistic and the creative, blue-collar labour, ancillary production, administration and so on. However, following on the example of US commercial network television (and before that the example of Hollywood), stations soon moved away from this model to outsourcing or 'farming out' much (although not all) production to independent producers and production companies. Under the contract-unit system, most employees were hired for the run of a production and were drawn from an industry-wide pool of labour. Instead of having a large, full-time permanent production staff, TV stations assigned a fixed budget to a programme, paying this to an independent producer. In turn, this 'packager' engaged staff and was responsible for the budgeting of other resources. Commercial TV operators eagerly embraced this development although ultimately the practice was also picked up by public service broadcasters. In turn, television stations moved to concentrate on a more singular role as broadcast distributors of programmes principally made available by others.

Now in the last ten to fifteen years comes a second major shift in the organization of the television programme content business. With the advent of the international trade in programme formats, the television industry shows signs of aligning itself with other service industries, most spectacularly those associated with fast foods but by no means restricted to this kind of service. Instead, the adaptable television programme has become a commodity of international trade and is now regularly achieving a kind of universal distribution never dreamed of before. In the past, most programmes had little circulation outside their country of origin. The major exception was those particular genres produced in the United States, most especially those of drama. Yet even then, this material was licensed as programmes in the can, ready for rebroadcast in another territory (admittedly with subtitles when that was necessary). The addition of the global TV format trade has meant that some programmes are now rendered as being highly adaptable. These come, not in the can, but in the form of the programme format package, ready for adaptation elsewhere. In turn, this form of distribution has assisted broadcasters in their search for less expensive forms of content made necessary in the face of new media distribution technologies and economic uncertainties. This has impacted sharply on more expensive genres including current affairs and drama series. In addition, with the mechanism of formats often being derived elsewhere, the development is also having serious repercussions for elements of independent local television production industries. Local programming may no longer mean output that is originated and produced locally. Instead with formats, production adaptation remains local although devising and development of formats may have occurred offshore. This, clearly, has important ramifications in terms of economics and culture although this is not the place to pursue such an analysis.

Instead, I concentrate here on the fact that in the present era, a new global type of television programme has emerged in the form of the format adaptation. This is truly a global form. Drawing upon but transforming older practices of transnational adaptation, the format is simultaneously international in its dispersal and local and concrete in its manifestation, a practice underlined and considerably strengthened by developments in the area of intellectual property. In turn, these changes lead to a situation of differentiated abundance in the contemporary era of television.

At a time when 'live' forms including reality shows, talent programmes and game shows have become mainstream, other forms such as drama series have become more marginal and less favoured.

It has been the task of this book to help in the understanding of this new development. As was suggested above, analysts and researchers have been slow to take account of this new phenomenon. Until 1998, for example, the only book on the subject of the television format was a legal handbook published in Dutch (van Manen 1994). There is no entry concerning television formats in the *New York Times Encyclopedia of Television* (Brown 1977) while only a short note appears in the first edition of the *Museum of Broadcasting Communication Encyclopedia of Television* (Fiddy 1997). Even in the realm of doctoral research, there is abundant silence. The only higher degree on the subject that I am aware of is a German study of the legal conditions of formats (Heinkeilein 2004).

That said, it is worth adding that there has been a good deal of passing critical notice paid to the redeployment of TV programme types from one place to another. These include several discussions of specific programme recyclings even if the researchers involved have not paid any conceptual attention to the general phenomenon of format adaptation (Heinderyckx 1993; Cooper-Chen 1994; Gillespie 1995; Pearson and Uricchio 1999; Miller 2000).

On the other hand, inside the international television industry, broadcasters and producers have been quicker in embracing the term and the concept. Indeed, the TV format is now a crucial mechanism in regulating the recycling of programme content across different television systems in the world (Cf. Heller 2003; Moran and Keane 2004). Thus, it is timely and appropriate that an English-language handbook on the subject of TV programme formats should appear. As was explained in the introduction, the book can be read by the general public and by the

TV industry alike for detail and insight as to just how this contemporary mode of television works. For the television industry, including those that seek to join it, these pages will, I hope, function as a guide, explaining at some length the different parts of the format industry and how these work together. Meanwhile, for the general reader, including those curious about what happens behind the television screen, the book has sought to furnish fuller and more precise knowledge, insight and understanding about this newest element of television's institution and culture. As the first appendix indicates, industry workshops and forums on the subject are starting to proliferate and the hope is that this book will be helpful for those running and participating in such events. It is surely time also that tertiary courses in mass communications and television also take seriously this new development so that I hope that *Understanding the Global TV Format* will prove useful for those engaged in critical research.

For this kind of reader, the book also works to introduce inquiries and debates that various researchers take up elsewhere (cf. Moran and Keane 2004; Heller 2003; Keane, Fung and Moran forthcoming). The fact is that just out of sight so far as formats are concerned are complex questions of history, matters of aesthetic and semiotic theory, issues relating to intellectual property, questions of copyright, changes in the institutional fields of media and business, matters affecting the commodification of culture, issues regarding technological transfer and so on. That these larger conceptual issues are not given sustained attention in these pages does not mean either that one is oblivious to these or that they are not regarded as important. However, as this book is a handbook that introduces the field to practitioners and others, the systematic analysis of these more theoretical matters is postponed to another time.

Nevertheless, in closing, it is worth adding some theoretical remarks by way of a postscript. Undoubtedly, the starting point for a more conceptual understanding of the area investigated here must concern the concept of the format. The very important point is not what it is but rather what it permits or facilitates (Moran 1998). And what it permits is, as has been seen, economic and cultural 'dialogue'. A key feature of formats is their binarism. For what they represent – to echo Neale writing about genre – are processes of systematization of difference within repetition (1980). They tie together the television system as a whole, national television industries, programme ideas, particular adaptations and individual episodes of specific adaptations. Hence, it is conceptually useful to realize that formats are in homological relationship with a series of other entities located at a set of crossroads where principles of difference intersect with principles of repetition. Put another way, alongside the phenomenon of the format and its adaptation we can include langue (/parole), genre (/text) and globalization (/local). All of these binary bundles appear to be *loci par excellence* of repetition and difference, sameness and variation.

Formats intervene between two levels of the production process within television institutions: that of mainstream programming at the macro level and the specific adaptation that finds expression in an individual text or programme episode at the micro level. They establish a regulation of the variety of mainstream programming across a series of individual programme episodes, organizing and systematizing the difference that each episode represents, filling the gap between the episode and the format as system. They are directly related to the textual economy of mainstream television programming in that they organize its regime of difference and repetition. In this way, they function to move the subject from episode to episode and from the level of the episode to the level of the programming system, binding these together into a constant coherence that is part of the television institution. In doing so, formats themselves are marked by difference within repetition - from one element of a format package to another, from one national adaptation of a format to another, from one series of a national adaptation to another series of an adaptation of the same format, and from one programme episode of the format adaptation to another.

In other words, formats are not so much systems as processes of systematization in which a rule-bound element and an element of transgression are equally important. In this respect there are clear analogies with genres and how they operate. Indeed, in stressing the multiple levels contained in an entity such as genre (or, for that matter, format), Lotman (1990) has coined the useful term 'incomplete equivalence' as a means of designating the necessary relationship between particular instances of the phenomenon or that obtaining between the level of the instance and the general level of the phenomenon. Just as there can be no such thing as a single example of a genre, say the film musical, that can contain all the different elements of the genre in a single film text, a kind of Ur text, so no single format adaptation can ever form the only possible or 'correct' rendering of a particular format and neither can any single adaptation ever comprise the range of possible renderings of that format.

This is an important conceptual point on which to end this book. Philosophically, there cannot be a 'correct' adaptation of a format. Instead, format adaptation always lies along a continuum ranging from the radically similar to the radically different. Some reversionings of a programme are easily spotted as translations whereas others are so different as to be almost completely unrecognizable. However, in making this distinction, we must also be prepared to realize that such a spectrum also lies along an axis of difference-within-repetition. Clearly, then, even beyond pragmatic understandings of formats that equip the reader to function effectively in the business and legal arenas of formats outlined here, there are many other conceptual matters that also invite inquiry.

APPENDIX 1
Further sources

Festivals, trade events and forums

Asia Television Forum, December, annual, Singapore. Platform for buying and selling of programmes.
Organization: Reed Exhibitions and Television Asia.
Available from: http://www.asiatvforum.com
E-mail: tony.chan@reedexpo.com.sg

Banff Television Festival, June, annual, Banff (Canada). Television festival and market.
Available from: http://www.bwtvf.com/

DISCOP, annual, East Europe. Annual content market for Central and Eastern Europe.
Organization: Basic Lead (Paris).
Available from: http://www.discop.com
E-mail: info@discop.com

Golden Rose, The (Rose d'or Festival), annual, Montreux (Switzerland). International market for formats, game shows and entertainment programming in general.
Available from: http://www.rosedor.ch/

MILIA, April, annual, Cannes (France). Publishing, new media and interactive multimedia market.
Organization: Reed Midem.
Available from: http://www.milia.com
E-mail: elizabeth.delaney@reedmidem.com

MIPTV, April, annual, Cannes (France). Major television market.
Organization: Reed Midem.
Available from: http://www.miptv.com/

MIPCOM, September/October, annual, Cannes (France). Films for television and television market.
Organization: Reed Midem.
Available from: http://www.mipcom.com
E-mail: peter.rhodes@reedmidem.com

MIPCOM Junior, held prior to MIPCOM, annual, Cannes (France). Specializes in children's television programmes.
Organization: Reed Midem.
Available from: http://www.mipcomjunior.com

NATPE, January, annual, USA. International market for television and specialist areas (digital media).
Organization: NATPE International.
Available from: http://www.natpe.org/

Protection, legal matters and advice

European Patent Office, available from:
www.european-patent-office-org/indexs.en.php
Established in 1973 as the outcome of the European countries determination to establish a uniform patent system. It provides information, newsletters and application forms for copyright registration. Thirty European countries are members of the EPO.

FRAPA (The Format Recognition and Protection Association), available from: http://www.frapa.org/.
FRAPA is an organization founded by television companies that collects now more than 100 companies. The aim is to provide a ground for a contractual system of regulation, of formats, protect television production and regulate legal disputes over format ownership.

German Patent and Trade Mark Office, available from: www.dpma.de/index.htm.
The site is in German language. It is the government copyright office website.

International Visual Communication Association, available from:
http://www.ivca.org/.
IVCA is a London based trade body for everyone involved in business media. Membership is essential. The organization represents commissioners, creatives and freelancers with production companies, government and other industry bodies. It offers a range of services, including recruitment, regular networking meetings, industry specific training courses and information resources.

The Patent Office, available from: www.patent.gov.uk/copy/.
It is the UK patent, copyright and trademarks office. It provides information and updates on copyright policy, complaints procedure and links to various copyright agencies.

US Copyright Office, available from: www.copyright.gov.
The website contains information, newsletters and key publications about copyright, and application forms for copyright registration. It also provides a direct link to an online database of copyright records since 1978.

World Intellectual Property Organization, available from: www.wipo.org.
The WIPO is the United Nations agency responsible for the protection of Intellectual Property. It contains comprehensive information about copyrights in the main countries and an online arbitration and mediation centre.

Worldwide Online Creator's Registry, available from:
http://www.worldwideocr.com/.
The Worldwide online creator's registry provides instant and affordable online copyright and intellectual property protection and archiving for creators internationally.

Trade publications and websites

BBC Commissioning, available from: http://www.bbc.uk.com/commissioning.
From this website it is possible to gather general information about working with the BBC, including the BBC code of practice and tariffs.

BBC Commissioning Public, available from:
http://www.bbc.co.uk/commissioning/structure/public.shtml.
This page is produced by BBC Commissioning. It provides information for the general public about getting in television or pitching ideas for new programmes.

BBC Commissioning Interactive, available from:
http://www.bbc.co.uk/commissioning/interactive/index.shtml.
From this site it is possible to gather information about how to submit proposals of interactive programmes. A form for interactive proposals and a TV format guide are available in PDF for downloads.

BBC Talent, available from: http://www.bbc.co.uk/talent/index.shtml.
This is a website specifically designed to look for 'raw' talents. Formal qualification and experience are not required. The site provides a monthly newsletter, available through registration.

Billboard, available from: http://www.billboard.com/.
Billboard is a newsweekly magazine of music, video and home entertainment. It is for the larger public, but also for professionals with its updates on sales, box-office grosses and reviews. Its online database contains weekly album, singles and video charts, reviews and special reports.

Broadcasting & Cable Magazine, available from: http://broadcastingcable.com/.
The news source on every aspect of the television industry. It covers the entire spectrum of broadcast, cable, satellite and multimedia. It is written for executives and provides links with industry partners.

C21 Media, available from: http://www.c21media.net.
C21 Media is an international publishing company specializing in television and media business and industry. It provides online reports, conferences and consultancy services as well as a database of news and features on content production, distribution and broadcast. The site's novelty is its online formats market that is easily accessible twenty-four hours a day. It is possible to book a 'virtual' stand in the market. C21 Media also publishes a yearly guide to television programmes' prices.

Hollywood Reporter, available from: http://www.hollywoodreporter.com/.
The trade publication for industry professionals for over 70 years. It includes news on film, television, home video and digital media.

Informamedia, available from: http://www.informamedia.com/.
Informamedia is part of the Informa & Telecoms Media Group. The organization has been supplying the media industry with business analysis since 1988. It provides management reports for the broadcasting, film and music industries, databases and links to events and training. It publishes the *Television Business International* magazine and the *TBI* yearbook.

International Review of Intellectual Property and Competition Law (IIC), available from: http://www.ip.mpg.de/Enhanced/Deutsch/Homepage.HTM.
The journal is published in English by the Max Planck Institute for Intellectual Property, Competition and Tax Law, Munich. Eight issues a year available through normal subscription or as a CD-ROM from the publisher.
The editorial office may be contacted at: iic@ip.mpg.de or via fax: +49-(0)89-24246-501.

Screendigest, available from: http://www.screendigest.com/.
London based organization that maintains a website with databases for research, business and analysis on global audiovisual media. It publishes a newsletter and an E-zine with the latest news on global television industry. The site provides online consultancy and organizes conferences and seminars worldwide. It requires membership.

Television Business International, available from:
http://www.informamedia.com/.
Now in its fifteenth year of publication, *Television Business International* (*TBI*) is a leading trade magazine for the international TV business, covering the production, distribution, broadcasting and financing of TV programming around the world.
In addition, the magazine's regular Television 2.0 section remains the industry's leading source of information on new media opportunities, from mobile applications to interactive TV developments.

TvFormats, available from: http://www.tvformats.com/.
TvFormats is a publishing and marketing company specializing in the organization of conferences and publications. It provides direct links with the major television companies dealing in formats.

Variety, available from: http://www.variety.com/.
Since 1905, *Variety* has offered news on the entertainment industry. It features a database of credits, global show business events calendar, classifieds, box-office charts, video-clips, event photo coverage and special reports.

Video Age International, available from: http://www.videoageinternational.com.
A monthly business journal of film, television broadcasting, cable, pay TV and other specialist areas. It is available through subscription and online. It participates at NATPE.

Vogue Planet, available from: http://www.vogueplanet.com/.
Vogue Planet is a Tokyo based media licensing and production. It concentrates on the production and distribution of formats in Japan with also the development of associated merchandising, brand licensing and e-commerce.

Training workshops and courses

Within the past three years, short practical workshops designed to introduce some of the principles and practices of format devising have sprung up in many different places. Australia, Denmark, Germany, Spain, and the United Kingdom are among numerous countries where these are reported as happening. One of the first was held in Dublin in October 2002 entitled Format Creation for Television Programming. We note some of its details as a typical example of what is happening in training and education and likely to snowball in the near future.

The course was mounted by Screen Training Ireland over three days and cost ?300. Industry needs was very much the driving force, particularly in the areas of creation and development. Applicants had to be nominated by a television or media company with whom they were working in the area of development. David Bodycombe (a game show specialist), John Gough (devisor and consultant to Distraction and handles public relations for the Rose d'Or Festival) and Chris Fuller (a freelance industry journalist) were the tutors.

The aim was to introduce participants to the principles of developing a programme idea into a television format with international potential. Topics included:

• Concept creation and generating ideas

• Case studies of successful TV Formats

• The business of TV formats

• Writing up proposals and paper formats

• International distribution

• Crossplatform applications

For further details contact Screen Training Ireland, available from: http://www.screentrainingireland.ie (see below). Among useful websites for searching details and locations of upcoming workshops, check the following:

NATPE, available from: http://www.natpe.org/.

The site provides access to the organization's databases of television information and worldwide industry news. NATPE organizes a national conference and exhibition and regional workshops and seminars. It also provides educational support offering grants, awards, training programs with industry partners and student career workshops.

Realityshowpitch.tv, available from: www.realityshowpitch.tv/.

This is an online scouting agency for television producers and production companies where writers and TV executives can pitch their reality TV shows ideas. It provides a database of original TV concepts. Writers can use the site to submit their series ideas to be reviewed by leading television production companies. It requires registration of membership.

Screen Training Ireland, available from: http://www.screentrainingireland.ie.

Screen Training Ireland provides training for professionals in film, television animation and digital media. Details about upcoming training programmes, Bursary Award scheme and a newsletter are available on its website.

Skillset, available from: http://www.skillset.org.

Skillset and the British Film Institute (BFI) run together a comprehensive database of media courses all over the United Kingdom.

The Skillset/BFI Course Database contains over 4,000 courses in film, television, video, radio and web authoring, and is regularly updated and checked for accuracy.

Appendix 2
'So, you want to create a game show?'

The document was downloaded from <u>http://www.tvformats.com</u> on 8 October 2004.

Format Creation

So, you want to create a game show?
A guide for the budding quiz devisor by games consultant *David J. Bodycombe*

This is a guide to game shows, intended to give advice to potential devisors who are interested in developing their ideas in this genre. The author, David J. Bodycombe, is a freelance consultant working in the UK, with experience in television, radio, books, magazines, newspapers, board games and the Internet.

The present Format Creation Guide has been published by www.tvformats.com, a Website dedicated to formats that currently does not exist anymore. However the following article gives you a good overview on how to devise a format. The original screenshots from different tv formats have been replaced for copyright reasons.

(i) Do your homework

A – Watch television!
Before you do anything, make sure you watch lots of game shows. Nothing will scupper your plans quicker than if, after weeks of development, you later discover that a nearly identical idea has already been on air for the past three years. This kind of situation has happened more than once before.

B – What's your genre?
Next, you'll need to decide what kind of genre you'd like to develop a show for. The genres of game shows have been fairly static over the year, and most programmes fall under one of these major headings:

Action/adventure – Typical elements of an action/adventure show include custom-made sports games, scavenger hunts, fantasy locations and role-play. Often played as a series of timed games, and personal betterment is often an underlying theme.

Board game conversion – Any sort of programme that has been based on a traditional or proprietary board game. In the latter case, this sort of show is only possible by paying a license fee to the manufacturer of the game.

Children's – Any form of programme specifically designed for children (approx. 16 years and under). Usually these programmes are commissioned from a separate department than that of adult and family light entertainment programmes.

Comedy panel game – Specific type of quiz or game involving a number of celebrity guests where a certain proportion of the material is pre-scripted and performed by the host or, in some cases, by the guests themselves.

Dating show – Shows concerning any aspect of personal relationships. Usually involves playing matchmaker to young contestants, although some recent shows have concerned themselves with how relationships fail.

Educational – Type of factual programming where a game element has been employed as a way of making the information fun to learn.

Family game show – Wide-ranging term used to describe mainstream primetime shows, usually presented by well-known comedians, where general knowledge is not a primary requirement. Often involves elements such as playing physical games, tactics and luck.

Lifestyle – Relatively new stream of programme taking a popular hobby or home interest, such as DIY or cookery, and basing an essentially light-hearted competition around it. Also includes shows where estimating prices is the key ability.

Panel game – Game played by a group of invited celebrities. Most of the humour comes from off-the-cuff remarks and banter, as opposed to the more scripted comedy panel games.

Puzzle – Show where lateral thinking, numerical ability and wordplay are important, but little or no general knowledge is required.

Reality – Where a number of individuals are challenged to work together as a team, usually over a long period of time.

Quiz, general knowledge – Game where answering a wide variety of questions is the key entertainment, although tactics and minor physical elements may also be present.

Quiz, themed – Show where contestants answer questions about a central theme. Often the rounds and games are also tied into this theme. Includes some themed panel games.

Sports – Programmes where a recognised sport is played, or the primary theme of the programme involves sport in some other way.

Stunt/dare show – Programmes where people are challenged to do extraordinary feats, usually involving expensive large-scale games or danger. Sometimes includes elements of practical jokes.

Technological – Specific genre where competitors construct machinery under competition conditions.

Variety – Programmes which either involve the search for new talent, or performances of established variety acts as a central element of the programme.

C – You, the critic
Once you know what kind of show(s) you're looking to devise, research into that genre more deeply. In particular, look at existing shows and critique them, asking questions such as:

- *What makes them tick?*
- *Is the pace fast or slow?*
- *At what time of day are these programmes usually shown?*
- *What kind of audience is it designed to appeal to?*
  Is it a mass audience or a particular niche? And what age group?
- *How does the scoring work?*
- *Is it played for prizes or just for fun?*
- *What type of host is used?*
-

(ii) Generate ideas

A – Any idea?
Next, you need to think of a basic idea around which your whole show will revolve. In essence, your idea needs to be two or three sentences that will sell the idea. If you can't encapsulate the idea succinctly, the chances are your idea is already too complicated.
Thinking of an original idea is very difficult to do. Quiz and game shows have been popular since the 1950s and in those 40-50 years many ideas have already come and gone. In our view, the two basic approaches are:

(i) Come up with something completely new. It can happen from time to time that a completely new idea occurs. One recent example was Channel 4's Fluke, which was almost an anti-game show in that the outcome of the whole programme purely depended on luck.

(ii) Do an old style show but in a modern way. What could be more boring than yet another multiple-choice quiz? But Who Wants To Be A Millionaire? has shown that you can take a simple idea and re-interpret it to give it some new dynamics. Some people argue that its not so much what the game show actually is, but whether it's executed well.

B – Some pointers
When thinking up your idea, try to bear in mind some basic principles:
Has anything similar been done before? If so, has it been at least several years since anything of a similar variety was broadcast?

Why would anyone watch your show? What makes it entertaining? Quite often, people assume that their job or hobby would make a good game show without considering that not everyone else might find their occupation or pastime interesting.

Is there a strong theme that will "brand" the show? In particular, is there a distinctive visual characteristic that will make the programme instantly recognisable?

Do you have a TV channel and time slot in mind?

Be realistic about costs. It's possible to achieve virtually anything in the world of television, but everything has its price. Can you honestly say that your idea will be able to be made on the kind of budgets used by similar shows in the marketplace at the target channel and timeslot?

Is the idea international? A sports quiz about the game of shinty might be great for Ireland, but its potential will be severely limited in the global marketplace.

C – Avoid the crowds

A number of themes are well worn, and you might want to steer clear of these unless you are convinced that you have a completely new angle. At the current time, some of the most often-used programme ideas seem to be:

- *Straightforward quiz shows involving questions, categories and amounts of money.*
- *Quiz shows that make use of clocks and collecting time.*
- *Quizzes or makeovers based on DIY, cookery or gardening.*
- *Children's shows that involve large inflatable obstacles and gunge.*
- *Word parlour games.*

Try looking for programme ideas that no one else seems to doing at the moment. Before too long, you may well find that the situation reverses to your benefit.

(iii) Refine, refine, then refine some more

A – Build it up then knock it down

Once you've structured your idea into a prototype format, you now need to refine the idea. From this point onwards, developing a game show is actually quite a destructive process. This is because you now need to look through the detail of your ideas and look for faults. Then, if possible, try to fix them.

B – Problems, problems

Here is a list of basic issues that need to be considered at this stage:

Cost effectiveness: From a television company's point of view, one of the main advantages of game shows over any other television programme is that they can be recorded back-to-back – that is, several shows are recorded in one day but are broadcast as a daily or weekly series. The longer your programme takes to film, the more expensive and complicated the production process gets and therefore it will appear less attractive to the marketplace.

Feasibility: There is a whole science to working out the technical practicalities of a programme, but there are some common-sense things you can check straight away. For example:

(i) If the show is studio-based, is it going to fit in a studio? Television studios are often a lot smaller than they appear to viewers, because cameras use wide-angle lenses that make the studio sets appear larger than they really are.

(ii) Does the set involve large mechanical constructions? Despite their appearances, studio sets are designed to be taken apart and re-assembled in hours. This is because studio time is so precious and expensive that its often more cost effective to re-build the set for each time you need it rather than leave the set sitting in the studio unused. For example, building an indoor rollercoaster within the studio would mean that the programme would probably have to be made within a large film studio – which can be hired out at weeks at a time – rather than in a traditional TV studio.

 Safety: Specialists are always consulted to ensure that the programme can be executed in a safe manner. However, even everyday obstacles such as ramps and stairs can be extremely hazardous. Other shows make a virtue of the aspect of danger. In these types of programmes it is vital that the audience can watch the programme safe in the knowledge that no one will come to any harm, particularly if it is for a family audience.

Live broadcasts: If the show relies on a live broadcast, bear in mind factors such as the time of year. This can effect the lighting and weather conditions. There is not much point hoping to get a live action-adventure show commissioned for evenings during Autumn if that means its going to be pitch black outside – the audience needs to see what's going on.

Game logic: If your programme is a quiz with a strong game element, check that the game really does work. If possible, get some of your friends to play an improvised mock-up of the game. Take note of how long it takes them to understand the rules. Does the strategy of the game reward contestants that take risks and play offensively rather than defensive, sandbagging play? A programme might be fun to play, but is it going to be interesting to the viewers? In particular, is there a "play-along" factor – that is, can the viewers try to answer the questions, games or puzzles before the contestants do?

"Filmability": Can the viewers see what's going on? Sets for all programmes are designed so that it is easy for cameras to capture the action. Sets come in many different forms, such as those used by Fifteen-to-One, Wheel of Fortune, Blind Date and Celebrity Squares. One thing to bear in mind is that most studios are not actually very high and so aerial shots are quite difficult to achieve.

Entertainment integrity: Does the format that you've now got actually fulfil the aim you started out with? It's often tempting to adjust your idea in order to solve some of the other problems that have occurred during the development process. However, a consequence of this is that your format might be very logical, cost-effective and technically feasible, but the original entertainment factor might have been lost.

The difficulty with the refining stage is that it's difficult to know what the pitfalls are. This is where agencies such as us can help. However, before you show your idea to anyone, it's advisable to secure your copyright on the format.

Writing and selling the format

A – Writing up your format
So, what does a format look like? Again, there are no hard-and-fast rules, but a very detailed description would give most of the information necessary to make the programme from scratch. There is no set length, but generally they do not extend much beyond 10 pages of A4 paper otherwise they appear intimidating to read. It may contain some or all of the following headings:

- *Programme title*
- *Target audience*
- *Suggested time-slot*
- *Length (mins)*
- *Brief outline (2-3 sentences)*
- *Outline running order*
- *Round structure (if applicable)*

- *Detailed synopsis*
- *Sample games/questions*
- *Illustrations*
- *Suggested presenters*
- *Outline budget*
- *Set design*
- *Merchandising opportunities*

Formats have been known to be accepted on a scrappy piece of typewriter paper, and even during a lunch conversation. However, conventionally it is preferred if the format is neatly printed by a word processor.

B – Approaching the market place

If you want to get a game show commissioned, there are four main ways of doing it:

i) – Independent production companies
These are private companies that make programmes for broadcasters. They live or die according to their success at winning commissions. Some broadcasters, such as the UK's Channel 4 and Channel 5, buy 100% of their programmes from independent production companies (or "indies"). To market your idea to an indie, you need to write to the head of light entertainment – whose details can be found in publications – and enclose your format(s). Most indies are generally very good at reading formats and supplying feedback. Sometimes they will ask you to sign a legal form that indemnifies them from any court action regarding the copying of your ideas. Companies do this because they often receive a number of formats that are nearly identical.

ii) – Directly approaching a broadcaster
Public service broadcasters, such as the BBC, welcome new ideas but are naturally reluctant to pay very much for them. Some commercially broadcasters will read ideas and can grant a provisional commission for good formats. However, you will still need to find an independent company to make the programme itself, although that's not too difficult if you already have a commission.

iii) – Use an agent
An agent will basically use the same two approaches listed above. The advantage is that agents will normally have more experience in negotiating contracts. Naturally, they will charge you a fee or a percentage of your income form the format for their services.

iv) – Format consultancies
Consultants are normally most interested in supporting of new talent, and will make a point of providing feedback on ideas and formats sent to them. They often provide additional services that can increase the chance of the format being sold. This might include commissioning professional illustrations, calculating a programme budget, or designing a prototype set.
Like agents, they will charge service fees and/or a percentage of income received for their services. Other areas of the tvformats.com site give further advice about how to protect your ideas and sell the format.

Good luck!

APPENDIX 3

Endemol Interactive Proposal Form

Date: _____

1) State name of initiative and company responsible contact details.

Name initiative: Company name: Contact person: Address: Phone: Fax: Email:

2) Give a brief business description, clearly describing products and services offered.

3) Define clear target group (volume, age, income, interests, industry, business size etc.).

4) Describe revenue model/income streams.

5) Describe the value chain and indicate which activities will be undertaken in-house.

6) Define required investments and largest ongoing cost components.

7) Give an overview and profile of main competitors.

8) Give a short description of how you see the role of Endemol related to your activities.

9) Please add a rough P&L for the first three business years.

[blank box]

10) Please note any other relevant information.

[blank box]

This form was accessed on 11/11/2004 at the following web address:

http://www.endemol.com/submit_proposal.xml

APPENDIX 4
Format companies (by region and country)

AFRICA

IVORY COAST
Cote Ouest (F).

NIGERIA
African Trumpet Telecommunications Nigeria Limited (F).

SOUTH AFRICA
Mountainside Media Pty Ltd. (F); Red Pepper Pictures (Pty) Ltd. (F).

ASIA

BRUNEI
Radio Television Brunei (F).

CHINA
Beijing Nsh Media Management & Consultant Co., Ltd. (F); China Television Media Ltd. (F); Huafeng Group Of Meteorological Audio & Video Information (F); Jade Media Co., Ltd. (F); Lutz Co., Ltd. / Trier Film & TV Ad. Co., Ltd. (F); Sichuan Television (F); Star Image Media Group (F); Yunnan TV China (F).

HONG KONG
Asia Pacific Vision (IF); Hong Kong Cable Television Limited (F); Typhoon Media International Limited (F); Walt Disney TV International Asia Pacific (F).

INDIA
Bennett, Coleman & Co., Ltd. (F) (IF); Miditech Pvt. Ltd. (F); Star India Pvt Ltd. (F); Zee Telefilms Limited (F); Optimystix Entertainment India Pvt Ltd. (F).

INDONESIA
Media Televisi Indonesia Pt (Metro TV) (F); Pt Cakrawala Andalas Televisi (ANTV) (F); Pt Cipta Tpi (F); Pt. Indosiar Visual Mandiri Tbk. (F) (IF); Rcti (F).

JAPAN
Ep Corporation (IF); Nippon Television Network Corporation (F); T.M. International, Inc. (F); Telesis International (F); Trans World Associates Inc. (F);

TV Asahi Corporation (F); TV Man Union Inc. (F); TV Tokyo Corporation (F); TV Tokyo Medianet Inc. (F); Yomiuri Telecasting Corporation (F).

KOREA (South)
A9 Media Inc. (F) (IF); CJ Media (F) (IF); Comedy TV (F); ITV (Kyungin Broadcasting Ltd.) (F); K2 Entertainment (F); KBS Media (F); MBC Production Co., Ltd. (F); Sun Media Co., Ltd. (F); Synergy Media Inc. (F); Telston Inc. (F); Xentervision Co. Ltd. (F); Youihl Entertainment (F).

MALAYSIA
Asa'ad Entertainment Network Sdn. Bhd (F) (IF); FE2 Productions Sdn Bhd (F); Firestar Media Sdn Bhd (F); Peppermint Asia Sdn Bhd (F); Sedania Corporation Sdn Bhd (F); Shasta Media Sdn Bhd (F) (IF); Silacom Sdn Bhd (F).

SINGAPORE
Media Authority Development Of Singapore (IF); Sph Mediaworks Ltd. (F); The Moving Visuals Co. Pte Ltd. (F).

SRI LANKA
Vanguard Management Services Pvt Ltd. (F).

THAILAND
Bec-Tero Entertainment Public Company Limited (F); Kantana Group Public Company Ltd. (F); Total Entertainment Marketing Co., Ltd. (F); United Broadcasting Corporation (F).

VIETNAM
Nhat Anh Advertising Co., Ltd. (F); Vietnam Television (F).

EUROPE

ALBANIA
Viziontrade (F).

AUSTRIA
ATV Privat-TV Services Ag (F); Blue Danube Media (Programme MEDIA) (F); Neue Sentimental Film Entertainment Gmbh (F).

BELGIUM
Endemol Belgie (F) (IF); Flanders Image/Flemish Audiovisual Fund (F); Jok Foe Nv (F); L&T Productions (F); MMG Nv (IF); Sputnik TV (F); Vrt (F); Woestijnvis Nv (F).

DENMARK
Adaptor D&D (IF); Frontier Media A/S (F); Koncern TV & Filmproduktion

(Programme MEDIA) (F); MTV Mastiff International (F) (IF); Saks Film Broadcast Aps (Programme MEDIA) (F); Skandinavisk Film Kompagni (F); STV Television (F); TV-Animation (F); TV Danmark A/S (F) (IF).

ESTONIA
Ruut (F) (IF).

FEDERATION OF RUSSIA
Amedia Studio (F); Rambler Broadcasting Limited (IF); Russian Pavilion/Joint Exposition Of Russian Studios (F); TNT – Network (F); Vid Entertainment Group (F).

FINLAND
Broadcasters Group (F); Magic Path Entertainment (F) (IF); MTV Oy (F); Sveng.Com Production Ltd. (F) (IF); Wireless Services Europe (F) (IF).

FRANCE
10 Francs (Programme MEDIA) (F); 2001 Audiovisuel – Groupe Telfrance (F); AB Groupe (F) (IF); Adventure Line Productions (F); Calt Productions (F) (IF); Compagnie Lyonnaise De Cinema S.A. (F); D.G.M.A (F); Dubbing Brothers (IF); Dupuis (IF); Ellipse Distribution (F); France Televisions Distribution (F); French TV (F) (IF); Glem (F); House Movie (F); Incontrolab (F); IPL (Programme Media) (F); La Huit (Programme MEDIA) (F); Ligne De Front (F); Limelight Films (F); Marvaud Olivier (F); Metropole Television (M6) (F); Moi, J'aime La Television (F); Mondofragilis Sarl (F); Ndrl Eiga (Programme MEDIA) (F); On Off (F) (IF); Pagnon Productions (F); Quai Sud Television (F); RDI Sas (F); Reservoir Prod. (F); Tele Images International (F) (IF); Thinktwice (F); Trace TV (F) (IF); Lagardere Images (F); Upside Television (F); Victorimage (F).

GERMANY
Beta Film Gmbh (F); Big Mag Media – Exciting Films Around The World (F); Constantin Entertainment Gmbh (F); Endemol Germany (F) (IF); FFK Kroehnert Gmbh (F) (IF); Filmpool Film (F); First Entertainment Gmbh (F); FRAPA – Format Recognition And Protection Association (F); German United Distributors Programmvertrieb Gmbh (F); Karmann Medienproduktion Gmbh (F); Media Luna Entertainment Gmbh & Co. Kg (F); Neue Deutsche Filmgesellschaft Mbh (F); Ohm: TV Gmbh (Programme MEDIA) (F); P2m Gmbh & Co Kg (IF); Radiate Entertainment Gmbh (F); RTL 2 Gmbh + Co. Kg (F); Schwartzkopff Tv-Productions Gmbh & Co. Kg (F); Seven Orange Media Ltd. (IF); Telcast Media Group (F) (IF); Telcomedia Consult Gmbh (F) (IF); Terzio Verlag Gmbh (IF); Time 2 Talk Show Gmbh (F); TV Link Gmbh (If); VR3 Virtual Production (F) (IF); Victory Media Gruppe (IF); ZDF – Zweites Deutsches Fernsehen (F) (IF); ZDF Enterprises Gmbh (F) (IF).

GREECE
A.D.D.P. Aslanis Ltd. (F); Antenna TV (F); Strada Productions (Programme MEDIA) (F); Tanweer Enlightenment Ltd. (F) (IF); Teletypos S.A. – Mega Channel (F) (IF).

HUNGARY
Telemedia Interactv Live Game Shows (IF).

IRELAND
Magma Films (F); Mind The Gap Films (Programme MEDIA) (F); Network Ireland Television (IF); Screentime Shinawil (F); Telegael (F).

ITALY
Ballandi Entertainment Spa (F) (IF); Einstein Multimedia Group Spa (IF); Endemol Italia/Aran Endemol (F) (IF); FBC Fact Based Communications Ltd. (F); Lumiq Spa (F) (IF); Millanta Film S.R.L. (Programme MEDIA) (F); Neo Network Srl (F) (IF); Palomar Spa (F); Princess Productions (IF); Rai Trade (F) (IF); Superpippa Channel – Edi On Web Srl (F); Union Contact, Srl. (F); Videodelta Spa (F); Videoshow Srl (F) (IF); Well Done Srl (IF).

NETHERLANDS
2waytraffic (F) (IF); Absolutely Independent (Programme MEDIA) (F); All3media International (F); Avro Broadcasting Association (F) (IF); Call Entertainment Europe Bv (F) (IF); Copyright Promotions Benelux (F) (IF); Endemol Bv (F) (If); Endemol Nederlands (F) (IF); Eye 2 Eye Media (Programme MEDIA) (F); Eyeworks TV (F) (IF); Fortune Formats (F) (IF); Harry De Winter Media (F); IDtv (F) (IF); Intellygents Bv (Programme MEDIA) (F); Joris Van Ooijen Media Concepten Bv (Programme MEDIA) (F); JVTV (Programme MEDIA) (F); MC&F Broadcasting Production and Distribution Cv (Programme MEDIA) (F); Media Republic (F) (IF); Novamedia B.V. (IF); Palazzina Productions B.V. (F); RTL / De Holland Media Groep (F); Stokvis & Niehe Producties B.V. (F) (IF); Swynk B.V. (F) (IF); TeVe Media Group (F) (IF); Toppop B.V. (Programme MEDIA) (F); Transmedia Communications (IF); Triple Seven Productions (Programme MEDIA) (F); Weijers Domino Productions B.V. (F) (IF); Yarosa Entertainment (IF).

NORWAY
Norwegian Film & TV Producers Association (F) (IF).

POLAND
Atm Grupa Sa (F); Endemol Neovision Sp.Zoo (F) (IF).

PORTUGAL
Endemol Portugal (F) (IF); Media Fashion (F) (IF); New Media Digital Contents, Lda (IF).

ROMANIA
Media Pro International (F); New Trend Media (IF); Sport Radio TV Media Srl.

SERBIA AND MONTENEGRO UNION
Nira F.T.C. (F) (IF).

SPAIN
3 Koma; Antena 3 Television (F); Boca Boca Producciones (F); Boomerang TV (F); Cedecom (Programme Media) (F); Elastic Rights (F); Europroducciones TV S.L. (F); Gestmusic Endemol (F) (IF); Globomedia (F); Grupo Pi (F); K-2000, S.A. (F); Malvarrosa Media (F); MIC Media Producciones Y Distributiones (IF); Microgenesis Producciones S.L. (F); Pausoka, S.A. (F) (IF); Radio Television Espanola Rtve (F); Retelsat, Sl (F); Selectavision (F); Sirius Media Solutions (F); Sonilab Studios (F) (IF); Televisio De Catalunya (IF); Tepuy (F) (IF); Urano Films (IF); Vision Europa (F); Vocento / SAS TV (F) (IF); Western Films (F); Xl Producciones Sl (Programme MEDIA) (F); Zeppelin Television (F) (IF).

SWEDEN
Baluba Ab; Bringiton Ab (F) (IF); Kamera Content Ab (IF); Metronome (F) (IF); Noble Entertainment (F); Plus Licens Ab; Titan Media (F).

SWITZERLAND
Faro TV (IF); New 7 Wonders (F) (IF); Regardez! Communications Gmbh (F); Ringier TV (IF); Rtsi-Televisione Svizzera (F).

UKRAINE
Inter TV Channel (F).

UNITED KINGDOM
19 Entertainment Limited (IF); 12 Yard (F); 3 Vision (Programme MEDIA) (F); All3media International (F) (IF); Angel Eye Scotland Ltd. (F) (IF); Ascent Media (F) (IF); Atomic Entertainment (IF); Avalon International (F); Barcud Derwen Associates; BBC; BBC Worldwide Ltd. (F); Blackwatch Productions Ltd. (IF); Bloomberg Television (IF); Blueshift Communications Llc (Programme MEDIA) (F); British Forces Broadcasting Service (F) (IF); British Home Entertainment Ltd. (Programme MEDIA) (F); Broadcast Marketing Ltd. (F); BSKYB Ltd. (F) (IF); Bullseye Distribution Ltd. (Programme MEDIA) (F); Cc-Lab (IF); Celador International Ltd. (F); Cellcast (F) (IF); Channel 4 International (F) (IF); Channel Television Limited (F); Chatsworth Television Ltd. (Programme MEDIA) (F); Chwarel (F); Cineflix International (F); CNBC Europe (F); Colstar International Television Ltd. (Programme MEDIA) (IF); Compact Collections (F); David Cuff Media And Commercial (F); David Finch Distribution Ltd. (F); Digital Matrix (F) (IF); DLT Entertainment UK Ltd. (F); Ealing Studios (F) (IF); Entara Limited (IF); Enteraction TV (IF); Entertainment Rights (F); Essential Film & Television (F); Extreme Entertainment (F); First Break Films (F); Five Television

(F) (IF); Flawless Media (F) (IF); Free Range Media (Programme MEDIA) (F) (IF); Fremantlemedia Ltd. (F); Gamer.TV (F); Granada (F); Granada International (F); Green Inc. Film & TV Ltd. (F); Hat Trick International Ltd. (F); Imago Productions Limited (Programme MEDIA) (F); Lewis Silkin (F) (IF); Lion TV Ltd. (F) (IF); Maitriconsulting Ltd. (F) (IF); Mark Rowland Ltd. (F) (IF); Marvel Enterprises International (F) (IF); MCG Programming (F); Mentorn (F); Minotaur International (F) (IF); No Strings Attached Ltd. (F); Novel Entertainment Limited (IF); NTL (IF); On-Air Systems (F) (IF); Optomen Television (F); Pact (F); Philip M Jones Associates (F) (IF); Presentable Limited (F) (IF); RDF International (F); Red Fig Limited (IF); Rosie Dixon Media (F); Screentime Partners Ltd. (F); Shine Limited (F); Silver Light (IF); Siriol Productions (F); Southern Star Sales Ltd. UK (F); Squash Post Production (IF); Storyland Ltd. (F); Tailor Made Films (F) (IF); Tape Consultancy Ltd. (F); Teledwyr Annibynnol Cymru (F) (IF); Television Corporation International (F); The Maidstone Studios (F) (IF); Tiger Aspect Productions (F); Touchdown Distribution (F); Turner Broadcasting System Europe Ltd. (IF); Twofour Productions Ltd. (F); Wales Screen Commission (F); Walestrade International (IF); Wall To Wall Television (F); Wark Clements & Co., Ltd. (IF); William Morris Agency (F); Winklemania Group (F); Zone Vision Enterprises Ltd. (F).

MIDDLE EAST

ISRAEL
FPAD – Middle-East Films, Footage, TV Formats Production & Distribution (IF); Israel Export Institute (F); Tel-Ad / Channel 2 (F); United Studios (F).

KUWAIT
Domino General Trading Co. (F) (IF).

LEBANON
Teleprog International (F); Elements TV (F).

SAUDI ARABIA
Al-Suhaimi Telemedia (F) (IF).

TURKEY
Atafilm A.S. (F) (IF); Fire Exit Productions (F) (IF); Ldi Lisans A.S. (F); Mediamax (F) (IF); Medyavizyon (F); Sera Film Services (F) (IF).

NORTH AMERICA

CANADA
Airwaves Sound Design Ltd. (F) (IF); Angel Entertainment (F); Canadian

Broadcasting Corporation; Societe Radio-Canad (F); Chalk Media Corp. (IF); Chocolate Moose Media Inc. (F); Chum Television International (IF); CMJ Productions (F); Conceptual Films Inc. (F) (IF); Creative Atlantic Communications Ltd. (IF); Distraction Formats (F); Ellis Entertainment (F); Fonds De Solidarite Ftq (F) (IF); Groupe Tva Inc. (F); La Fete (F) (IF); Lone Eagle Entertainment, Ltd. (F); Mediatique Inc. (F); Octant Vision Inc. (IF); Pip Animation Services Inc. (F) (IF); Portfolio Entertainment Inc. (F); Pure TV / Group Pram (F); Sunspot Media Inc. (F) (IF); The May Street Group (F); Title Entertainment Inc. (F) (IF); Tricon Films & Television (F); Trinome Inc. (IF); Vivavision (F).

UNITED STATES
A Paravision Inc. (F); Academy Entertainment, Inc. (F); Animation World Network (IF); Belinda Noah Productions, Inc. (F); Blueprint Entertainment (F); Broadway Video Enterprises (F) (IF); Cable Ready (F); CBS Broadcast International (F); Cinamour Entertainment (F); Court TV (F); Dragon Head Ventures (F) (IF); EEMC (IF); Endemol USA (F) (IF); Eyewitness Kids News International (F); Eye Television (IF); Food Network (F); Foothill Entertainment, Inc. (F); Fremantle Corporation (F); GDC Entertainment (IF); Happy Face Entertainment (IF); ICM (F); IFC Companies (F); License! Magazine (IF); Lions Gate Entertainment (F); Michael Hoff Productions, Inc. (F); MTG Media (F); Newmagic Communications, Inc. (F); Playboy TV International (F); Productions On The Parkway, Inc. (F); Pump Audio Llc (IF); Salsa Entertainment (F); Sandy Frank Entertainment (F); Scout Productions (F); Scholastic Entertainment (IF); Sunbow Entertainment (F); Supersonic Communications (F); Teleproductions International (F); Televisa Estudios (F); The Gurin Company (F) (IF); True Entertainment (F) (IF); Venevision International (F); World Of Wonder Productions, Inc. (F); Worldwind Entertainment, Llc (F) (IF).

OCEANIA

AUSTRALIA
Australian Children's Television Foundation (F); Beyond Distribution Pty Ltd. (F); Blue Rocket Productions Pty Ltd. (IF); Circling Shark Productions (F); Goldrim Media (F) (IF); Halo Pictures (IF); International Entertainment Services P/L (F) (IF); Intomedia (F); Kapow Pictures (IF); Mumbo Jumbo Animation Pty Ltd. (F); Southern Star (F); Verve Entertainment (F) (IF); WBMC (F) (IF); Xyznetworks Pty Limited (F).

NEW ZEALAND
Greenstone Pictures (F); Ninox Television (F); Touchdown Television (F); TV3 Network Services Ltd. (F); TVNZ – Television New Zealand (F) (IF).

SOUTH AMERICA

ARGENTINA
Abaplus (F) (IF); Cuatro Cabezas S.A. (F); Endemol Argentina (F) (IF); Promofilm Sa / Globomedia (F); Telefe International (F).

BRAZIL
Endemol Globo (F) (IF); Globosat Programadora Ltda (F); Radio E Televisao Record S/A (F); TV7 Video Comunicacao Ltda (F) (IF).

CUBA
Cumago Caribe S.A. Media (F).

MEXICO
Television Metropolitana Sa De Cv Canal 22 (F); TV Azteca S.A. De C.V. (F).

References

Adair, D. and Moran, A. (2004), 'At The TV Format Coalface: Mark Overett and David Franken In Conversation', *Working Papers In Communications*, 2, Brisbane: Griffith University, pp. 24–8.

Alesandro, K. (1997), 'Pilot Programs', in H. Newcomb (ed.), *Museum of Broadcasting Communication Encyclopedia of Television*, Chicago: Fitzroy Dearborn, pp. 1258–60.

Alvarado, M. and Buscombe, E. (1978), *Hazel: The Making Of A Television Series*, London: British Film Institute.

Anonymous, no date, 'Canada dips its toe into formats', http://207.68.164.250/cgibin/linkrd?_lang=EN&lah=4967dd7442a74c4304f67ef8528904dc&lat=1045607454&hm___action=http%3a%2f%2fwww%2ec21media%2enet%2ffeatures%2ffeat_dtl%2easp%3fid%3d5482%26t%3d6. Accessed 19 February 2003.

Anonymous, no date, 'Formats Present and Future', (2002), http://www.distraction.com. Accessed 18 February 2003.

Anonymous, 'Globo Announces Alliance with Endemol', (2001), www.broadcastingandcable.com. Accessed 11 April 2003.

Anonymous, (1994a), 'Endemol's Top Formats And Programs', *Television Business International*, August, pp. 23–24.

Anonymous, (1994b), 'World Of Difference', *Moving Pictures*, October, p. 68.

Anonymous, (1995), 'First Class Travels With Auntie', *The Times*, 1 March, pp. 35–6.

Anonymous, (2002), 'Middleman? Ben Silverman Helped Sell "Millionaire", "Weakest Link"', *Wall Street Journal*, 18 May, p. 98.

Anonymous, (2002a), 'The Bold Return of Mr Light Entertainment if Paul Jackson has his Way', 'Saturday nights in Kazakhstan will never be the same again', *Financial Times*, 23 July, p. 44.

Anonymous, (2002b), 'The Reality after the Show: Endemol', *The Economist*, 14 September, pp. 64–5.

Anonymous, (2002c), 'Cash Corp', *The Guardian*, July 22. http://www.guardian.co.uk. Accessed: 15/9/2003.

Anonymous, (2003), 'The future is red: Gaming channel Avago shows the potential for interactive TV ventures', *Financial Times*, 21 January, p. 2.

Armer, A. A. (1998), *Writing the Screenplay: TV and Film*, Belmont: Wadsworth Publishing Company.

Australian Broadcasting Corporation (2003), 'Four Corners TV Program Transcript', abc.net.au http://www.abc.net.au/4corners/stories/s335957.htm. Accessed: 20/5/2004.

Bart, P. (2000), 'Surreal "reality" puts world in format hell', *Daily Variety*, 269: 26, 10 September, p. 23.

BBC WorldWide, www.bbcworldwide.com. Accessed 11 April 2003.

BBC WorldWide Annual Review, http://www.bbcworldwide.com/review/tvsales_and_formats.html. Accessed 11 April 2003.

Beauchamp, C. and Behar, H. (1992), *Hollywood On The Riviera: The Inside Story of the Cannes Film Festival*, New York: W. Morrow and Co.

Bell, N. (1994), 'Major Man', *Television Business International*, April, pp. 19–23.

Bellamy, R. V., McDonald, D. G. and Walker J. R. (1990), 'The spin-off as television program: form and strategy', *Journal of Broadcasting and Electronic Media*, 34, pp. 283–297.

Bellamy, R. V. and Trott, P. L. (2000), 'Television Branding as Promotion', in S. Eastman, (ed.), *Research in Media Promotion*, Mahwah: Lawrence Earlbaum Association, pp. 127–159.

Berland, J. (2003), 'Radio Space and Industrial Time', in L. Justin, and T. Miller, (eds.), *Critical Cultural Policy Studies: A Reader*, Oxford: Blackwell, pp. 230–39.

Blumler, J. and Nossiter, T. (1991) (eds.), *Broadcasting Finance in Transition: A Comparative Handbook*, New York: Oxford University Press.

Bodycombe, D. (2002), 'So you want to Create a Game Show: A Guide for the Budding Quiz Devisor', http://www.tvformats.com/formatsexl2lained.htm. Accessed: 20/3/2005.

Borglund, M. (2002), Interview with Albert Moran, Sydney.

Brenton, S. and Cohen, R. (2003), *Shooting People: Adventures in Reality TV,* London and New York: Verso.

Briel, R. (2001), 'If you Cannot Join them, Beat them', *Television Business International*, 17 August 2001, p. 179.

Brooke, A. (1995), Interview with Albert Moran, London.

Brown, L. (1977), *The New York Times Encyclopedia of Television*, New York: New York Times Press.

Brunsdon, C., Johnson, C., Moseley, R. and Wheatley, H. (2001), 'Factual entertainment on British television: The Midlands Research Groups 8–9 Project', *European Journal of Cultural Studies*, 4, pp. 29–62.

Brunt, R. (1985), 'What's My Line?', in L. Masterman, (ed.), *Television Mythologies*, London: Comedia, pp. 21–28.

Buneau, M. A. (2000), 'When is a Format not a Format?', *Television Business International*, February, pp. 44–50.

Buneau, M. A. (2001), 'Up For The Prize?', *Television Business International*, January/February, pp. 25–28.

Burnett, K. (2002), 'To Have and To Own', *Television Asia's Guide to Formats*, Singapore, Television Asia, p. 9.

Burnett, M. (2001), *Dare to Succeed: How to Survive in the Game of Life,* New York: Hyperion.

C21 Media, http://www.c21media.net. Accessed: 23/11/2004.

Campbell, B. (2003), Interview with Albert Moran, Sydney.

Carlton, http://www.carltonplc.co.uk/carlton/about/. Accessed 11 April 2003.

Castaway Television Productions Ltd v. *Endemol Entertainment International,* 27 June 2002 – unpublished in English.

Celador Productions Ltd v. Danmarks Radio (2000) E.C.D.R. 158.

Celador, www.celador.com.uk. Accessed: 15/11/2004.

Chafee, Z. (1945), 'Reflections on the Law of Copyright', *Columbia Law Review*, 45, pp. 503, 513–514.

Chatterbox Productions (2004), www.ampersandcom.com/chatterbox. Accessed: 18/2/2005.

Christie, J. (2003), Interview with Albert Moran, Auckland.

Chuck Blore and Don Richman Inc. v. *20/20 Advertising* 674 F. Supp 671 (1987).

Coltman, M. C. (1988), *Franchising in the US: Its Pros and Cons*, Vancouver: Self-Counsel Press.

ConAgra Inc. v. *McCain Foods (Aust) Pty Limited* (1992) 23 *Intellectual Property Reports* 193.

Constantakis-Valdes, P. (1997), 'Computers in Television', in H. Newcomb, (ed.), *Museum of Broadcasting Communication Encyclopedia of Television*, Chicago: Fitzroy Dearborn, pp. 412–13.

Cooper-Chen, A. (1994), *Games in the Global Village: A 50-Nation Study*, Ohio: Bowling Green University Popular Press.

Coopman, J. (2000), 'Euros to Studios: Send in the Clones', *Variety*, 20 January 2000, pp. 8, 161.

Cousins, B. (2002), Interview with Albert Moran, London.

Cozens, C. (2003), 'Test the Nation Heads Stateside', http://www.bbc.co.uk. Accessed 21 January 2003.

Cramp v. *Smythson* (1944) Appeal Cases 329.

Cunningham, S. and Jacka, E. (1996), *Australian Television and International Mediascapes*, Melbourne: Cambridge University Press.

Curtin, M. (1996), 'On Edge: US Culture in the Neo Network Era', in R. Ohmann, (ed.), *Marketing and Selling Culture*, Case Western Reserve: Wesleyan University Press, pp. 181–203.

Daswani, M. (2002), 'Managing Risk: Broadcasters are betting on the success of affordable, lowrisk formats, while distributors are looking for novel ideas to keep the genre fresh', *World Screen*, July, http://www.worldscreen.com/featuresarchive.php?filename=managingrisk.txt.Accessed: 3/3/2004.

Dawley, H. (1994), 'What's in a Format?', *Television Business International*, November, pp. 24–6.

Deans, J. (2002), 'Pop Idol creator may pocket $10m from US sale', *Financial Times*, 18 February, p. 43.

Dicke, T. S. (1982), *Franchising in America, 1840–1980: The Development of a Business Method*, Chapel Hill & London: The University of North Carolina Press.

Dill, C. E. (2003), 'The History of "travellers": Recycling in Prime Time American Network Programming', in *Journal of Broadcasting and Electronic Media*, 47: 2, pp. 260–279.

DISCOP (2004), www.discop.com. Accessed: 15/2/2005.

Distraction (2003), http://www.distraction.com/corporateprofile.asp?nav_id=192&lang_id=E. Accessed 18 February 2003.

Elliott, P. (1972), *The Making of a Television Series*, London: Constable.

Endemol (2002), profile section 'Endemol History' from Endemol Presskit, http://www.endemol.com/press_kit.xml. Accessed 30 December 2002.

Endemol (2004), 'Endemol boosts creativity with Global Creative Team', http://www.endemol.com. Accessed 28 June 2004.

Eyeworks TV, http://www.eyeworks.tv/. Accessed 22 January 2003.

Eyeworks (2002), 'National IQ Test 2002 Gives Antena 3 Major Boost', Press Release 17 December 2002, http://www.eyeworks.tv. Accessed: 12/2/2003.

Feist Publications Inc. v. *Rural Telephone Service Co. Inc*. 499 U.S. 340 (1991).

Fiddy, D. (1997), 'Format Sales, International', in H. Newcomb, (ed.), *Museum of Broadcasting Communication Encyclopedia of Television*, Chicago and London: Fitzroy Dearborn Publishers, pp. 623–24.

Frean, A. (1995), 'Have I Got A Show For You', *The Times*, 12 October, p. 23.

Fine, F. L. (1985), 'A Case for the Federal Protection of Television Formats: Testing the Limit of "Expression"', *Pacific Law Journal*, 17, pp. 49–67.

Flew, T. (2002), *New Media: An Introduction*, Melbourne: Oxford University Press.

FRAPA (2003), http://www.frapa.com. Accessed: 15/10/2002.

Freeman, M. (2002), 'Forging a Model for Profitability', *Electronic Media*, 21, pp. 13–15.

Fremantlemedia (2003), http://www.fremantlemedia.com. Accessed 11 April 2003.

Frith, S. (1987), 'Copyright and the Music Industry', *Popular Music*, 71. pp. 57–75.

Fuller, C. (1994a), 'Soaps Success Shows No Sign of Abating', *Television Business International*, 16 April, pp. 23–4.

Fuller, C. (1994b), 'CLT in Talks with Endemol', *Broadcasting*, 16 December, p. 12.

Gillespie, M. (1995), *Television, Ethnicity and Cultural Change*, London and New York: Routledge.

Gitlin, T. (1985), *Inside Prime Time*, New York: Pantheon Books.

Glori, U. (2002), 'Speech', *The Netherlands Fourth Annual TV Meets the Web Seminar*, 16–17 May, Royal Tropical Institute, Amsterdam.

http://www.tvmeetstheweb.com/may2002/speakers.php. Accessed 30 December 2002.

Goldsmith, C. (2001), 'Brash U.S. Agent Helped Spark British TV Invasion: Who Wants to be a

Goodwin, P. (2001), 'The Winning Formula', *TV World*, July-August, pp. 29–30.

Gough, L. (2002), 'The drama over format rights', *Managing Intellectual Property*, 119, pp. 26–30.

Granada (2003), http://www.granada.co.uk . Accessed 11 April 2004.

Grantham, B. (2003), Interview with Albert Moran, Brisbane.

Green v. Broadcasting Corporation of New Zealand (1989) 16 *Intellectual Property Reports* 1.

Griffiths, A. (2003), *Digital Television: Business Challenges and Opportunities*, London: Palgrave.

Gross, L. S. (1997), 'Cable Network', in H. Newcomb, (ed.), *Encyclopedia of Television*, Chicago: Fitzroy Dearborn, pp. 265–271.

Hansen, G. (2002), Interview with Albert Moran, Sydney.

Hazelton, J. (2001), 'The Third Way', *Television Business International*, April, p. 76.

Hartog, S. (2003), Interview with Albert Moran, Fremantlemedia, London.

Hazelton, J. (2000), 'Remade in the USA', *Television Business International*, October, pp. 51–6.

Heinderyckx, F. (1993), 'Television News Programmes in Western Europe', *European Journal of Communication*, 8: 4, pp. 425–50.

Heinkeilein, M. (2004), *Der Schutz der Urheder von Fernsehshows und Fernsehshowformaten*, Baden Baden: Nomos Verlagsgesellschaft.

Heller, D. (2003), 'Russian "sitcom" adaptation: the Pushkin effect', *Journal of Popular Film and Television*, 31: 2, pp. 60–86.

Hobson, D. (1982), *Crossroads: The Drama of a Soap Opera*, London: Metheun.

Hyatt, W. (1987), *Encyclopedia of Daytime Television*, New York: Billboard Books, p. 364.

Idato, M., (2004), "Steal the show", Press clipping supplied by email by David Franken.

Inglis, K. (1982), *This is the ABC*, Melbourne: Melbourne University Press.

Jarvis, C. (1996), Interview with Emma Sandon, London.

Johnson-Woods, (2002T), *Big Bother: Why Did That Reality TV Show Become Such A Phenomenon?*, Brisbane: University of Queensland Press.

Keane, M., Fung, A. and Moran, A., forthcoming, *Out of Nowhere: Television Formats and the East Asian Cultural Imagination*, Hong Kong: Hong Kong University Press.

Kingsley, S. (2003), 'Formats for Success', (quoting Anna Bråkenhielm, managing director of Strix Television), http://www.frapa.org/Coverage/success.htm. Accessed 17 February 2003.

King World, (2004), http://www.kingworld.com/aboutKWP.htm. Accessed: 15/2/2004.

Lane, S. (1992), 'Format rights in television shows: law and the legislative process', *Statute Law Review*, 13, pp. 24–49.

Lawson, A. (2002), 'Independent Television Does It Tough', *The Australian*, 17 October, pp. 17

Lee, L. T. (2004), 'Formats', in C. Sterling, (ed.), *Encyclopedia of Radio*, Chicago and London: Fitzroy Dearborn Publishing, pp. 612–14.

Levine, J. (2003), 'Sex, Money & Videotape', *Forbes*, 17 March, pp. 86–9.

Lewis, J. (1998), 'How do you go about creating a hit television quiz show? Here's an interview with a man who knows', Channel 4, http://www.channel4.com. Accessed: 15/9/2004.

Liddiment, D. (2002), 'Formatting The Future of TV Entertainment', Speech at Forum on Formats, Mipcom, (2005), www.reedexpo.com/'app/PrintFriendly.cfm?K_MT_ID=182&moduleid = 574&K_MAG_ID=1480&step=FullStory&appname=100266. Accessed: 15/1/2005.

Lotman, Y. (1990), *Universe of the Mind: A Semiotic Theory of Culture*, Bloomington: Indiana University Press.

Malbon, J. (2004), Interview with Midas Productions, Dublin.

Mapplebeck, V. (1998), 'The Mad, the Bad and the Sad', *DOX*, 16, pp. 8–9

Mathijs, E. and Jones, J. (2004) (eds.), *Big Brother International: Formats, Critics and Publics*, London and New York: Wallflower.

McChesney, R. W. (1999), 'The New Global Media', *The Nation*, 269: 18, 29 November, pp. 11–15.

Meade, A. and Wilson, A. (2001), 'Oh Brother, What's Next?', *The Australian*, 19 July, p. 33.

MILIA, (2004), http://www.milia.com. Accessed: 7/11/2004.

Miller, J. (2000), *Something Completely Different: British Television and American Culture*, Minneapolis: University Of Minnesota Press.

MIPCOM, (2003), http://www.mipcom.com. Accessed: 7/11/2004.

MIPTV 2003, http://www.miptv.com. Accessed: 20/9/2003.

Moran, A. (forthcoming), *Make It Australian: Transnational Television and National Culture*, Sydney: University of New South Wales Press.

Moran, A. and Keane, M. (2004), 'Joining the Circle', in A. Moran, and M. Keane, (eds.), *Television Across Asia: Television Industries, Programme Formats And Globalization*, London and New York: Routledge-Curzon.

Moran, A. (2001), 'International TV Program Format Industry, 1997/2001', Report for IsICult (Istituto Italiano per l'Industria Culturale).

Moran, A. (2000), 'Travelling Templates and National Fictions: The Restless Years in Europe', in J. Weiten, G. Murdock, and P. Dahlgren, (eds.) *Television Across Europe: A Comparative Introduction*, London: Sage, pp. 84–93.

Moran, A. (1998), *Copycat TV, Globalization, Program Formats and Cultural Identity*, Luton: University of Luton Press.

Moran, A. (1989), 'Three Stages of Australian Television', in G. Turner, and J. Tulloch, (eds.), *Australian Television: Programs, Pleasures and Politics*, Sydney: Allen and Unwin, pp. 1–14.

Moran, A. and Keane, M. (2005), 'Street Life: British, German and Chinese Adaptations of a Fiction Format', *Media International Australia*, University of Queensland, Brisbane, forthcoming.

Murray, S. and Ouelette, L. (2004) (eds.), *Reality TV: Remaking Television Culture,* New York: New York University Press.

NATPE,(2004), http://www.natpe.org. Accessed: 8/9/2004.

Neale, S. (1980), *Genre*, London: British Film Institute.

Nicols v. *Universal Pictures Corp.* 45 F.2nd 119 (1930).

Nintendo of America Inc v. *Elcon Industries Inc.* (1982) 564 F. Supp. 937.

Noam, E. (1992), *Television in Europe*, New York: Oxford University Press.

Norowzian v. *Arks Ltd* No. 2 (2000) No. 2, EMLR, 67.

NRW (Government of Northern Westfalia, Germany)/FRAPA, Press Release (nd).

Overett, M. (2002), Interview with Albert Moran, Brisbane.

The Oxford English Dictionary (2nd edn.) (1989), vol. VI, Oxford: Clarendon Press, p. 85.

Paterson, C. (1997), 'Satellite', in H. Newcomb, (ed.), *Museum of Broadcasting Communication Encyclopedia of Television*, Chicago: Fitzroy Dearborn, pp. 1438–39.

Pearson, R. A. and Uricchio, W. (1999) (eds.), *The Many Lives Of The Batman*, London and New York: Routledge.

Penhaligan, L. (2002), 'In Brief – UK', *Copy World*, No. 119, p. 9.

Perkin, C. (2001), 'It May Be Real Life But It's Death For Drama', *Sydney Morning Herald*, 15 July, p. 49.

Perkin v. *Ray Bros* (1911), Macg. Cop. Cas. 288, p. 13.

Reyher v. *Children's Television Workshop*, 533 F.2nd 87 (1976).

Rodrigue, M. (nd), 'Formats Come of Age', Distraction Formats Flyer.

Rodrigue, M. (2002), Interview with Albert Moran, London.

Rogers, M. C., Epstein, M. and Reeves, J. S. (2002), '*The Sopranos* as HBO Brand Equity: The Art of Commerce in the Age of Digital Reproduction', in D. Lavery, (ed.), *This Thing of Ours: Investigating* The Sopranos, New York: Columbia University Press, London: Wallflower Press, pp. 42–57.

Rose, D. (1999), 'Format Rights: A Never-ending Drama (or not)', *Entertainment Law Journal*, p. 170.

Roth, D. (2000), 'Real World Creator: Some Reality Bites', *Fortune*, 142: 4, 14 August, p. 38.

Saenz, M. (1997), 'Programming', in H. Newcomb, (ed.), *Museum of Broadcasting Communication Encyclopedia of Television*, Chicago: Fitzroy Dearborn, pp. 1301–08.

Sanghera, S. (2002), 'UK export a hit with American audience: Television US Version of "Pop Idol" Biggest Show On Fox TV', *Financial Times*, 5 September.

Shrover, S. (1997),'Telcos', in H. Newcomb (ed.), *Encyclopedia of Television*, Chicago: Fitzroy Dearborn, pp. 1630–31.

SPADA News (Screen Producers and Directors Association of New Zealand) (2002), quoting Geoff Steven, TVNZ Head of Programme Development in the format and entertainment genre, No 68, May 2002.

Spot-on (1999), OLG Munchen, ZUM, p. 244.

Stevens, G. (2003), Interview with Albert Moran at TVNZ, Auckland

Strix, http://www.strix.se/. Accessed 11 April 2003.

Thompson, K. (2003), *Storytelling in Film and Television*, Cambridge, Mass.: Harvard University Press.

Thompson, K. (1999), *Storytelling in the New Hollywood: Understanding Classical Narrative Technique*, Cambridge, Mass.: Harvard University Press.

Todreas, T. M. (1999), *Value Creation and Branding in Television's Digital Age*, London: Quorum Books.

Tulloch, J. and Moran, A. (1986), *A Country Practice: Quality Soap*, Sydney: Currency Press.

Turan, K. (2000), *Sundance To Sarajevo: Film Festivals and the World they Made*, Berkeley: University of California Press.

Tyreell, P. (2002), 'TV companies launch a different play for today: Interactive Television', *Financial Times*, 18 September, p. 15.

van Manen, J. (1994), *Televisieformats: en-iden nar Nederlands recht*, Amsterdam: Otto Cranwinckle Uitgever.

Vaughan, C. L. (1979), *Franchising: It's Nature, Scope, Scope, Advantages, and Development*, Massachusetts and London: Lexington Books.

Walker, S. (2001), 'Branding the World', *Television Business International*, January/February, pp. 52–6.

Westcott, T. (1995), 'A Family Affair', *Television Business International*, February, pp. 18–22.

Who Wants to be a Millionaire? (2002), http://millionaire.itv/com/millionaire/home.php. Accessed: 20/11/2002.

Wieten, J., Murdock, G. and Dahlgren P. (2000), *Television Across Europe: A Comparative Introduction*, London and New York: Sage.

The Wit, (2001), 'The Format Business: (Desperately) Looking For Zero Risk', *SIS (Strategic Information Services) Briefings,* European Broadcasting Union, No. 44, November 2001.

Wood, D. (1999), 'Life In The Old Daytime', *Broadcasting*, 11 November, p. 29.

INDEX